Ages 2–5

TOP 50

Updated **Instant**

Bible Lessons

for Preschool

TOP 50 INSTANT BIBLE LESSONS® FOR PRESCHOOLERS

© 2016 by Rose Publishing, LLC

Published by RoseKidz®
An imprint of Hendrickson Publishing Group
Rose Publishing, LLC
P.O. Box 3473
Peabody, Massachusetts 01961–3473 USA
www.hendricksonpublishinggroup.com

Cover Illustrator: Chad Thompson

CONDITIONS OF USE

Scriptures taken from the Holy Bible, New International Reader's Version®, NIrV ® Copyright © 1995, 1996, 1998, 2014 by Biblica, Inc.™ Used by permission of Zondervan. www.zondervan.com The "NIrV" and "New International Reader's Version" are trademarks registered in the United States Patent and Trademark Office by Biblica, Inc.™

ISBN: 978-1-62862-497-7
RoseKidz® reorder# R50002
RELIGION/Christian Ministry/Children

Printed in the United States of America
Printed February 2020

Contents

Introduction

This is your one stop for the top 50 Bible stories each child should know. This full year of lessons takes your young ones through the Bible in an age-appropriate way. Volunteer friendly activities using easy to find materials makes prep a snap. You can easily adapt these lessons to Sunday school, children's church, Wednesday night bible study, Christian school classroom or your family home. And because there is a variety of reproducible ideas from which to choose, you will enjoy creating a class session that is best for your group of children.

How to Use This Book

Each chapter includes a Bible story, Memory Verse, Application Questions, and up to 4 activities to help reinforce the truth in the lesson. This gives you options to adjust what you do with the children in your class according to their levels of interest and ability and the amount of time you have with them. Each activity is fully reproducible and comes with: materials list, step-by-step directions, and what to say to further the learning.

Teaching children is exciting and rewarding—especially when you are successful in hiding God's Word and its principles in the hearts of your children. Instant Bible Lessons will help you accomplish that goal. Blessing to you as you serve our Lord and Savior in this most important way.

Each Lesson Includes

Age-Appropriate **Memory Verse**

Read-Aloud **Story to Share**

Engaging **Discussion Questions**

Materials—Everything you need to lead activities

Preparation—What to prepare before the kids arrive

Directions—Simple-to-follow and volunteer friendly

What to Say—Reinforces Bible truths being taught

Chapter 1
God Creates the Earth and Us

Memory Verse

You are the children that God dearly loves.
So follow his example. Ephesians 5:1

Story to Share

When God decided to create the earth, he worked
on it for six days. God wanted it to be beautiful—
and it was! God used the color blue to create the sky
and the oceans. He included lots of green when he
created grass, trees, and flower stems. He colored the
ground and tree trunks brown. Then God splashed
a bit of color everywhere when he made red, purple, yellow, orange, and pink flowers.

God loved the colorful earth. He said, "It is good." The earth
was full of color, and God wanted people to help him enjoy the
beautiful world. "I will make a man—in my image," God said.

He called the man Adam. God did not want Adam to be alone, so he made a
woman, Eve. God made Adam and Eve to enjoy the world he had created. Adam
and Eve did what God told them to do and took care of the plants and animals.

God made us to be like him so that we could love him and be his friend. He loves us
and wants to be our friend. Just like Adam and Eve, God wants us to take care of the earth.

—*based on Genesis 1 and 2*

Discussion Questions

1. What does God want us to do with the earth?
2. What can you do when you see trash in your neighborhood?

Garbage Police

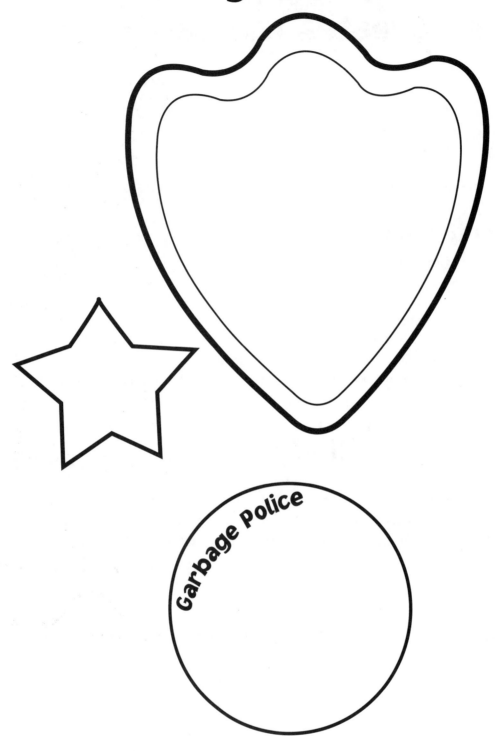

Garbage Police

Materials: • copies of this page, one for each child • scissors • aluminum foil
• crayons • safety pins • transparent tape • paper or plastic bags

Preparation: Cut out a set of badge pieces for each child. Using star pattern, cut one large star from aluminum foil for each child.

Directions: 1. Children write their names on the "Garbage Police" circle. 2. Children glue the stars and "Garbage Police" circles on the badges. 3. Tape a safety pin to the back of each badge. 4. Pin a badge on each child. 5. Give a paper or plastic bag to each child. Take a walk around the church grounds to pick up garbage.

What to Say: You can help take care of the earth by picking up trash you see on the ground. Remember when you are finished with a gum wrapper, soft drink can, or tissue to hold it until you are near a trash can. God wants us to keep the earth beautiful.

Verse Picture

You are the
children that
God dearly
loves. So follow
his example.
Ephesians 5:1

Materials: • copies of this page, one for each child • small buttons • glue • fabric scraps • construction paper
Directions: 1. Show how to make a child on the picture using a button face, fabric scraps for clothes, etc.
2. Children glue picture on a sheet of construction paper to make a frame.
What to Say: Repeat the memory verse several times with the children.

Hearts and Flowers Garden

Materials: • copies of this page, one for each child   • scissors   • butcher paper   • crayons   • glue

Preparation: Cut out a flower, stem, leaves, and heart for each child. Post a large piece of butcher paper on a wall. Draw large trees on the paper.

Directions: 1. Children color their flowers, petals, and stems. 2. Help children write their names on the hearts. 3. Show children how to glue the stems to the flowers. 4. Assist children to glue the flowers and hearts to the butcher paper to create a garden scene. 5. Write the memory verse along the bottom. 6. Children sit in front of the "garden" during story time.

What to Say: The hearts in our garden remind us that God loves us!

Beautiful Things

God made beautiful things . . .

. . . and God made me!

Materials: • cut or torn pictures of creation from magazines • glue • construction paper

Directions: 1. Provide a piece of construction paper for each child. 2. Instruct them to pick out their favorite pictures of creation and glue them on to their paper. 3. At the top, print "God made beautiful things." At the bottom print, "and God made me!"

What to Say: Look at all the beautiful and different things God has made. They are all different colors and sizes. The favorite thing God made was you and me. He made each of us beautiful and different.

Chapter 2
Seventh Day of Rest

 **Memory Verse**

Remember to keep the Sabbath day holy. Exodus 20:8

 Story to Share

In the beginning of time, there was nothing. There was no land, there were no stars or sun, and there were no animals or people. There was just darkness. God was in the heavens and said, "Let there be light." Now there was light and darkness—day and night. That was the first day of creation.

On the second day, God made the sky, creating the heavens.

On the third day, God made the oceans, the seas, and land. He made trees, plants, and flowers. The earth became beautiful.

On the fourth day of creation, God made the sun and moon. Then he made the stars to shine at night.

On the fifth day God filled the water with fish and the air with birds. Now the splashing fish could be heard along with the singing birds.

On the sixth day God made animals that roar, grrr, and baa. He made animals that hop, animals with long necks, and animals with stripes. He loved all his creation, but he still wanted a special friend. So God created a man made just like himself.

God really worked for six days. He looked at all the things he had made and he was happy. "Yes," God said. "This is very good."

One more day was left in the week. The world was made, the animals were made, man was made. "I will bless this day," God said. "This will be the day to rest. This will be the day all those on Earth can worship and praise me."

God rested on the seventh day; it was the first holy day.

—based on Genesis 1:1—2:3

Discussion Questions

1. How many days did God give us to work? To rest?
2. What is the best thing you can do on the day of rest?

Church Time!

Remember to keep the Sabbath day holy.

Exodus 20:8

Materials: • copies of this page, one for each child • crayons

Directions: Children draw a picture of themselves going to the church and color the rest of the picture.

What to Say: Look at the people going to church. They are respecting God's holy day by going to his house to worship him.

Creation Cards

Materials: • copies this page, one for each child   • scissors   • crayons   • paper clips

Preparation: Cut out one set of cards per child.

Directions: 1. Children color the cards. 2. While you tell the story, children put their cards in order. 3. Help children paper clip each set together to take home. Encourage children to tell the story to someone at home.

Suggested Usage: Make the story cards available for early-birds to color before class.

Pillow Pals

God is
watching over
_____

Materials: • copies of this page, one for each child • scissors • cotton balls • glue • crayons
Preparation: Cut out the bunny patterns.
Directions: 1. Children color the bunny front. 2. Children glue three cotton balls on the back of the bunny front and then glue the bunny back to the other side. 3. Children glue a cotton ball to the bunny's back for a tail.
Suggested Usage: This is a good time to reassure children that while God rests, he does not sleep. **While you are sleeping, God will be watching over you.** Place your pillow pal on your pillow to remind you he is taking care of you.

Seven Finger Play

1, 2, 3, 4, 5, 6,
days God worked.

**Hold up counting
fingers.**

Making light
and flowers
and monkeys.

**Pretend to smell
a flower.**

But on day 7 God rested.

Hold up seven sign.

Just like me.

Lay head on hands.

Materials: • colored copies of this page, one for each child • scissors • craft sticks • glue **Optional:** • curling ribbon • yardstick • scissors
Preparation: Cut out a large 7 for each child. **Optional:** Cut one 14-inch length of ribbon for each child and curl ribbon ends on scissors.
Directions: 1. Children glue the 7 to the end of a craft stick. **Optional:** 2. Children glue the curled ribbon around the stick at the bottom of the 7.
What to Say: With children, practice motions shown above. Lead children in repeating the words, doing the motions, and holding up the 7 as shown.

Chapter 3

Adam and Eve Sin

Memory Verse

God did say, "You must not eat the fruit from the tree in the middle of the garden." Genesis 3:3

Story to Share

Adam and Eve were in a beautiful garden. They were in charge of all the plants and animals. They loved God and each other. God gave them only one rule. They could not eat the fruit from the tree in the middle of the garden called the tree of knowledge of good and evil (Genesis 2:17). God said if they did eat the fruit, they would die!

One day when Eve was near the tree in the middle of the garden, a serpent started to talk to her. "Did God really say, 'You must not eat the fruit of any tree that is in the garden'?"

The woman said to the serpent, "We can eat the fruit of any of the trees that are in the garden, accept the tree that is in the middle of the garden. God told us if we did, we would die."

The serpent lied to her and said. "You won't die, you will learn new things." Eve saw the fruit looked good to eat. So she took some of the fruit and ate it. She also gave some to Adam, and he ate it, too!

All of a sudden they realized they had no clothes on, and so they hid. They hid from God. God called out to them, "Where are you? You have eaten the fruit from the tree that I forbid you to eat from, didn't you?"

Eve pointed to the serpent and said, "He told me to."

Adam pointed at Eve and said, "She told me to!" God was angry and made them leave the beautiful garden forever. He made the serpent slide around on his belly forever like a snake.

God was sad that Adam and Eve had sinned. When we sin, we separate ourselves from God. God didn't want to be separated from them, but Adam and Eve had made the choice to sin. God wants us to obey him so we can stay close to him. You can choose to do right things and make God happy.

—based on Genesis 3

Discussion Questions

1. **Who did Eve listen to?** (The serpent.)
2. **What happened when they ate the fruit?** (They were separated from God and had to leave the garden.)
3. **Do you follow the rules your parents give you?**

Spiral Snake

Preparation: Cut yarn into 10-inch lengths, making one for each child.

Directions: 1. Each child colors their snake. 2. Assisting as needed, children cut on the lines to create the spiral snake. 3. Use hole punch to punch a hole at the end of the snake's tail. 4. Assist children to tie a length of yarn through the hole, forming a loop from which to hang the snake.

What to Say: Just like Adam and Eve we have rules that God wants us to follow. Sometimes we don't listen like when Adam and Eve listened to the serpent. We can make God happy and follow the rules.

Follow the Leader

Directions: 1. Children line up to play "Follow the Leader." 2. Lead for a while and then select a volunteer to be the leader.

What to Say: When God tells us what he wants us to do we should follow him. When we play our game, the leader is going to show us the way to go and we are going to follow them.

Forbidden Fruit

God said, "Do not eat from this tree!"

(See Genesis 3:3.)

GOD   FORGIVES   ME

Materials: • copies of this page, one for each child • scissors • hole punch • yarn
Directions: 1. Children color the fruit and tree and cut them out. 2. Help the children punch holes in apples and tree, and use yarn to tie the apples to their tree.
What to Say: God gave Adam and Eve one rule to follow. Not to eat from one tree. We all sometimes make bad choices. When we do we can ask God to forgive us for those bad choices. Hang your tree up at home to remind you to ask God to forgive you when you do wrong things.

Smiley-Face Signs

paper plate (front)
paper plate (back)

Materials: • copies of this page, one for each child • scissors • small paper plates • glue • craft stick

Directions: 1. Copy a set of happy and sad faces for each child. 2. Children color happy and sad faces. 3. Assist children to cut out faces. 4. With your help, children glue a craft stick to the bottom of the plate, and then glue one picture on each side of the plate.

What to Say: Adam and Eve did something very wrong. They disobeyed God. We make good and bad choices, too. We are going to talk about some decisions. You show me if it is a bad choice or a good choice. Read the following list of choices. Pause after each example, allowing time for children to respond. **Picking up your toys.** (Smiley face) **Yelling at your mom or dad.** (Sad face) **Helping others.** (Smiley face) **Showing love to your family.** (Smiley face) **Throwing a fit.** (Sad face) **Not listening.** (Sad face) **Obeying your mom and dad.** (Smiley face) **Smiling.** (Smiley face) **Pushing or hurting someone.** (Sad face) As time allows, continue with statements of your own.

Chapter 4
Cain and Abel

Memory Verse

When you are angry, do not sin. Ephesians 4:26

Story to Share

After God sent Adam and Eve out of the Garden of Eden because they had sinned, they set up a new home. They had a son named Cain, then they had another son named Abel.

Adam and Eve taught the boys to work. Abel became a shepherd and took care of the sheep. Cain liked to farm the fields, growing grain and fruit.

Adam and Eve worshiped God by making an altar to him. They made the altar from stones, and they brought only their best offerings to the altar. Adam and Eve taught Cain and Abel to make offerings to God, too.

On one offering day, Abel, the shepherd, chose a perfect lamb to bring to God. He had looked carefully at all his sheep. He wanted to give God the very best.

Cain, the farmer, also brought an offering to God. He took some of his fruit and grain, and brought it to the altar for God.

God was pleased with Abel's offering. He joyfully accepted the offering. But when God saw what Cain brought to him, God was not pleased.

Cain pouted and said to his brother, "God likes you best."

God saw him pouting and asked, "Why are you pouting? All I want you to do is obey."

But Cain was still angry. He found Abel in the fields, caring for the flock. Cain then killed Abel because he was jealous of him. God punished Cain by sending him from his home and gardens.

God does not want us to be jealous of others. He wants us to be happy!

—*based on Genesis 4:1–16*

Discussion Questions

1. Why was Cain jealous of his brother, Abel?
2. How should you feel when a friend gets a new bike or game?

Cain and Abel

Materials: • copies of this page, one for each child • scissors • crayons • glue • cotton balls • transparent tape
Preparation: Cut out one set of pictures for each child.
Directions: 1. Children color the pictures. 2. Give each child a stretched cotton ball to glue to Abel's lamb. 3. Help the children tape their cutouts back-to-back. 4. Assist each child in gluing the correct clothes on Cain and Abel.
What to Say: Retell the Bible story as children use their cutouts to act out the story.

Cain and Abel Maze

Abel

When you are
angry, do not sin.
Ephesians 4:26

Materials: • copies of this page, one for each child • crayons **Optional:** • clear Con-Tact paper
Preparation: Optional: To use the sheets more than once, cover them with clear Con-Tact
paper. When the children are finished, simply wipe off the crayon marks.
Directions: Give each child a maze and a crayon.
**What to Say: Your crayon is going on a journey. Everyone start with Abel, then go to each picture
when I say it. You will end up at our memory verse, in the Bible.** Re-read the Bible story while the children
complete the maze. Then read the memory verse, encouraging the children to repeat it with you.

Wonderful Worship

Materials: • copies of this page, one for each child plus one extra • crayons

Directions: Children color their pages.

What to Say: Lead children to point to the appropriate pictures as you point and lead them in the following activities: Point to the story book and retell the story. Point to the children singing and lead children in singing "Jesus Loves Me." Point to the children praying and pray a short prayer of praise. Point to the Bible and lead children to repeat the memory verse. Boys point to the boy at the bottom and girls point to the girl as you lead children to say, **We will worship God with our best.** Close, saying, **Both Abel and Cain wanted to worship God. Abel took his best. Cain brought an offering that didn't please God. Let's always give God our best!**

The Best Lamb

Materials: • copies of this page, one for each child • crayons • cotton balls • glue

Directions: 1. Children color their pictures. 2. Children glue cotton to the lamb without a mark on it.

What to Say: Abel chose the best lamb to give to God. Can you find the lamb without a mark? When we give offerings to God, he wants our best, too. He wants us to give him ourselves. We need to eat good food, exercise our bodies, and get plenty of sleep. Then we can give him our best.

Chapter 5
Noah

Memory Verse

God blessed Noah and his sons. Genesis 9:1

Story to Share

God was sad. People were acting very badly. So God said, "I will send a flood to get rid of all the bad things. First I will find a man who loves me and is good. I will have him build an ark to save himself and the animals."

God chose Noah and his family. Noah was a godly man. He was without blame among the people of his time. He walked with God.

Noah had three sons. Their names were Shem, Ham, and Japheth. God said to Noah, "Build an ark. Bring two of every living thing into the ark. Bring male and female of them into it. They will be kept alive with you."

Noah did everything exactly as God commanded him. He loaded all kinds of food for the animals and his family. Everyone had a place to sleep, eat, and live. Noah talked to his sons and said to get their wives packed and ready to go. Noah and his family went into the ark.

Then it began to rain. It rained for 40 days and 40 nights. God kept Noah and his family and all the animals safe inside the ark.

When the flood started to dry up, Noah sent out a bird to see if there was land. The bird came back with a piece of tree. Noah knew there was dry land for them to leave the ark and start a new life. God told Noah it was time to leave the ark.

Noah was thankful that God took care of them. God promised to never send a flood like that again. To show he would keep his promise, God made a beautiful rainbow in the sky.

—*based on Genesis 6:9—9:17*

Discussion Questions

1. How many of each animal did Noah take into the ark?
2. What did God put in the sky to help us remember his promise?

Noah Stand-Ups

Materials: • copies of this page and page 29, one of each for each child   • scissors   • resealable plastic bag   • transparent tape

Preparation: Cut out ark, Noah figures, and animals. Place a set of all figures in a plastic bag, making one set of figures for each child.

Directions: 1. Help children fold the ark in half to make it stand up. 2. For each of the figures, children fold the tabs to the back and with assistance tape tabs to form a ring for the figures to stand.

What to Say: Retell the Bible story, using the stand-up figures and ark to act out the story. Children follow your actions with their own figures and ark. When you stand up the ark, leave the opening large enough for the figures to fit inside. Scoot animal figures inside the ark as you tell about Noah gathering the animals. Then have Noah go inside. At the end of the story, remove Noah stand the animals. Children place figures and ark inside plastic bag to take home.

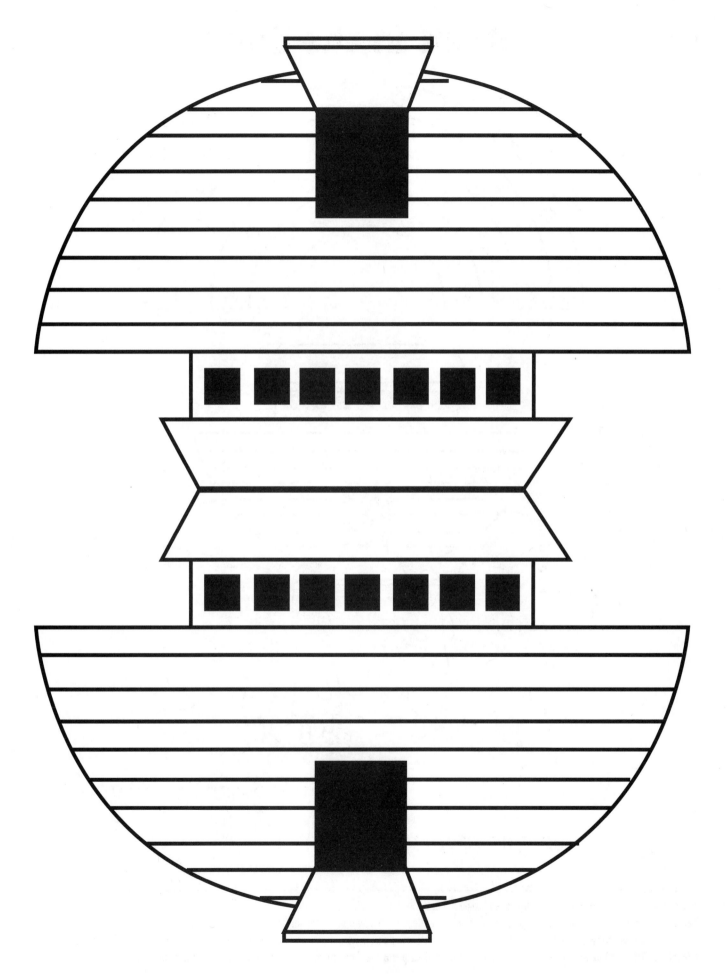

What's in the Sky?

◇ = red   O = yellow

✝ = orange   ⛵ = green

Materials: • copies of this page, one for each child • crayons
Directions: 1. Read the story from page 27 to the children. 2. Help the children color in the rainbow
with the corresponding colors. 3. While the children color their pictures, retell the story.
What to Say: What do we find? Yes, it's a rainbow. God put a rainbow in the sky to remind us of his promise.

Two of Every Kind

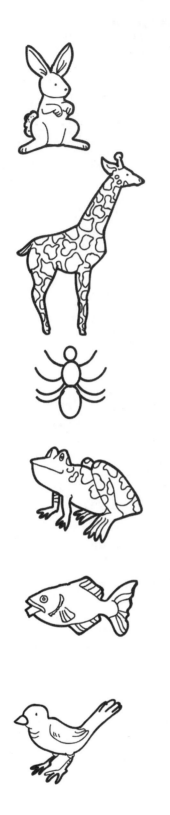

Materials: • copies of this page, one for each child • crayons
Directions: Children draw a line from one animal to its match.
What to Say: Matching these animals reminds us that God told Noah to take TWO of every animal inside the ark.

Chapter 6
Abraham Has a Son

 ## Memory Verse

Be patient. James 5:7

 ## Story to Share

Abraham was a man that loved God. He chose to do just what God told him to do. God was happy with Abraham and made him a promise.

"I will make our people a great people, Abraham. I will bless you and make your name great. Everyone here on earth will be blessed because of you."

They traveled to where God told them to go. God said to him, "Abraham, I will give all this land to your children." Abraham was old and his wife was old. He wondered how God would give the land to his children if he didn't have any. He was too old to have children now.

God spoke to Abraham, "Look up, Abraham. See all the stars in the sky?"

Abraham looked at the twinkling stars in the sky.

"Yes, Lord, there are many, many stars."

"You will have many in your family," promised God. "You will have children, your children will have children, and those children will have children. You will have more descendants than the stars in the sky. This land, Canaan, will belong to them."

Abraham knew God always keeps his promises. After God promised them a son, they had to wait a long time. It was hard for Abraham and Sarah to wait for their son, but Abraham had patience. When Sarah was 90 years old she became pregnant and they had a son. They named him Isaac.

—*based on Genesis 15:1–6*

 ## Discussion Questions

1. Do you like it when your mom or dad says, "Just a minute?" Why?
2. Do you think you should learn to be patient now so when God wants you to wait you will find it easier to be patient?

Hidden Stars

How many stars can you find in the picture?

Materials: • copies of this page, one for each child • scissors • flannel • yellow crayons
Preparation: Cut a small piece of flannel for each child.
Directions: 1. Children color the stars with a yellow crayon 2. Children glue the flannel on Isaac's blanket.
Suggested Usage: Have this activity ready for those extra minutes while you are preparing for another activity. (There are 30 stars in the picture.)

Patient Books

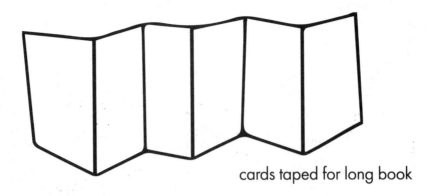

cards taped for long book

Materials: • copies of this page, making one book cover for each child • 4x6-inch plain index cards • transparent tape • scissors • glue
• star stickers and/or star stamps and stamp pads

Preparation: For each child, fold three index cards in half. Open the cards and tape them together at the sides
to form a long book (see above). Write "God's Promise to Abraham" along the bottoms of the books.

Directions: 1. Children cut out a book cover for each child. 2. Show the children how to glue the book cover to the front. 3. Children fill their book
with stars: use star stickers and/or star stamps and stamp pads. 4. Count with the children to see how many stars they have in the skies of their books.

What to Say: God makes promises to you, but you must be patient and wait. He promises you a beautiful home in Heaven. What
are some other promises of God?

Finish the Picture

Draw: ☑ a tent behind Abraham ☐ five stars in the sky ☐ a moon in the sky ☐ Abraham's face.
When you're done drawing, color the picture.

Be patient. James 5:7

Materials: • copies of this page, one for each child • crayons
Directions: Children follow instructions to complete the picture.

More Than All of These

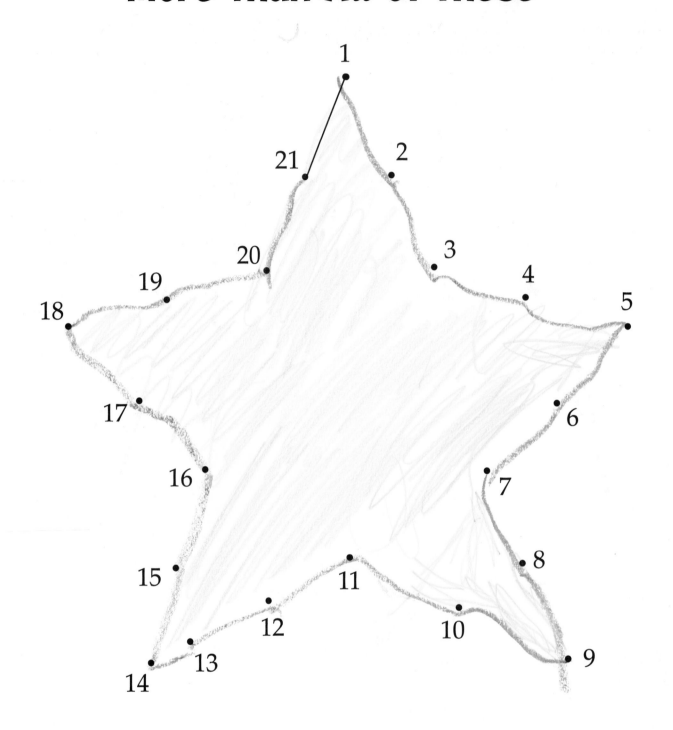

Be patient. James 5:7

Materials: • copies of this page, one for each child • crayons
Directions: Children complete dot-to-dot puzzle and then color page.
What to Say: God told Abraham he would have more family than all the stars!

Chapter 7
Jacob and Esau

Memory Verse

Don't lie to one other. Colossians 3:9

Story to Share

Esau and Jacob were twins. Esau was the oldest twin, so he would inherit their father's special blessing. This was a very big honor. Not only would the oldest son get many of his father's things when he died, but he also would be the leader of the family.

The two brothers were opposites. Esau was his father Isaac's favorite son. He liked to hunt in the woods.

Jacob was his mother, Rebekah's, favorite. He liked to stay near home.

Jacob knew that Esau would get their father's blessing. He wished that he had been born first.

"Mother, why?" he would ask with a jealous heart. "Why can't Father give me the blessing?"

"Son," Rebekah would say, "You know the oldest son receives the blessing. But don't worry, I have a plan."

Rebekah and Jacob planned to trick his father, who was blind, into giving the blessing to Jacob instead of Esau. One day while Esau was out hunting deer for his father's dinner, Rebekah prepared a meal for Jacob to give to his father. Because Esau's arms were hairy and Jacob's were smooth, Rebekah took a goatskin and wrapped it around Jacob's arms.

The trick worked! When Isaac felt Jacob's hairy arms and smelled the delicious meat dish, he thought Jacob was Esau. So he gave Jacob the blessing.

Jacob took what wasn't his, because he was full of jealousy instead of love for his brother. He later was punished for not being honest.

—*based on Genesis 27:1–20*

Discussion Questions

1. Do you ever lie to get what you want?
2. How does that make God feel?
3. What can you do when you feel like lying?

Bible Story Pictures

Materials: • copies of this page enlarged by 150 percent, one for each child • scissors • crayons • masking tape

Preparation: Cut out a story set for each child.

Directions: 1. Children color the pictures. 2. Make loops of masking tape and place on the backs of Jacob and Esau figures. 3. As you retell the Bible story, children use the story set to act it out.

What to Say: Jacob and Esau liked different things. What did Jacob like? (Staying close to home, the tent) **What did Esau like?** (Hunting) **What are some differences between you and other people in your family?**

Sneaky Snake

Materials: • colored copy of this page • scissors

Preparation: Cut out snake.

What to Say: Satan came to Eve in the form of a snake. We sometimes say that someone is "as sneaky as a snake." We're going to play a game that will remind you to be honest instead of sneaky like Jacob was.

Directions: 1. Children sit in a circle to play a game like Duck, Duck, Goose. 2. Choose one volunteer to be "Jacob." 3. "Jacob" walks around the outside of the circle and drops the snake behind another child while saying, "Sssssssnake!" 4. That child then stands up and tries to tag "Jacob" before "Jacob" gets around the circle and back to the empty place to sit down. 4. If caught, "Jacob" takes another turn and the running child returns to the empty seat. If "Jacob" sits before being tagged, the running child becomes the new "Jacob."

Do Not Lie Sign

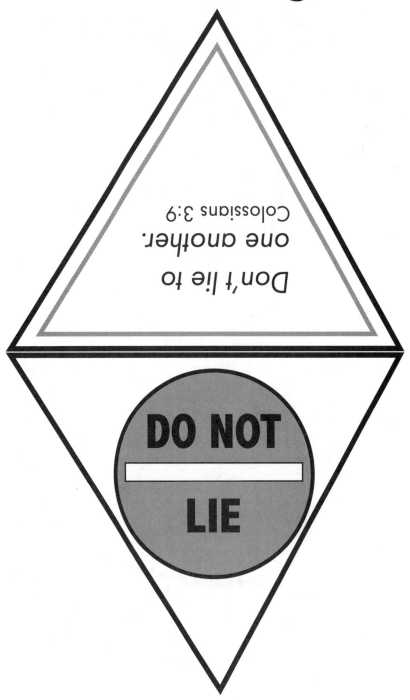

Don't lie to
one another.
Colossians 3:9

DO NOT
—
LIE

Materials: • bright yellow copies of this page, one for each child • scissors • glue • craft sticks
Directions: 1. Children cut out the signs, keeping the two pieces together along the middle. 2. Children fold signs in half, sandwich one end of a craft stick between the pointed ends, and glue the front and back of the sign together. 3. Children hold up their signs and say, "Do not lie." Then turn the signs around and quote the verse.
What to Say: Have you ever seen a sign along the road that said, "Do not enter"? If the person driving the car disobeyed the sign, they could have an accident. The sign is there for a reason. Our sign says, "Do not lie." God's command is for a reason. If you disobey it, bad things could happen!

Who Is It?

Isaac

Jacob

Rebekah

Esau

Materials: • copies of this page, one for each child • red, blue, purple and green crayons

Directions: 1. Read the "Who" questions below as children answer the questions together. 2. Help the children use the correct colors to answer the questions.

What to Say:
- • Who was the daddy of Jacob and Esau? Draw a circle around him with a green crayon.
- • Who was the mommy of Jacob and Esau? Draw a circle around her with a blue crayon.
- • Who was the brother who liked to hunt? Draw a circle around him with a red crayon.
- • Who was the sneaky brother? Draw a circle around him with a purple crayon.

Chapter 8
Baby Moses

 ## Memory Verse

Serve one another in love. Galatians 5:13

 ## Story to Share

God's people were in the land of Egypt.
Their families grew and grew.

Pharaoh said, "We must do something to
keep these people from becoming so strong
that they can rule over us." So, the king made
God's people become their slaves. Then, he
said that all baby boys must be killed so there
would be no more generations of God's people.

Moses' mother put Baby Moses in
a basket on the Nile River. Moses' sister
Miriam watched to make sure the baby was safe. Pharaoh's daughter found the
basket in the bulrushes (tall water plants). When she opened it, she saw the baby. He
was crying. She felt sorry for him. "This is one of the Hebrew babies," she said.

Miriam asked Pharaoh's daughter, "Would you like
me to get someone to feed the baby for you?"

When Pharaoh's daughter said yes, Miriam left and got her mother. Moses' mommy
got to help take care of him, and he was safe. When the child grew older, his mother
took him back to Pharaoh's daughter, and he became her son. She named him Moses.

Miriam, Moses' sister, had helped God by helping her
family. She helped keep her baby brother safe.

based on Exodus 1:8—2:10

 ## Discussion Questions

1. What was in the basket that Miriam's mother put in the river? Baby Moses.
2. Who did Miriam find to help Pharaoh's daughter take care of baby Moses? Moses' mother.

Baby Moses Story Figures

Materials: • one copy of this page enlarged by 150 percent • scissors • construction paper, brown or green • pencil

Preparation: Cut the three pictures from the page. Prepare the bulrushes: fold a sheet of brown or green construction paper in half, then fold it in half again. Use scissors to cut strips down from the open side (not the folded sides), down to approximately 1 inch from the bottom. Use a pencil to curl the strips outward to look like grass or bulrushes.

Directions: 1. As you tell the story, hold the bulrushes piece upright. 2. Slip the baby Moses figure between the folds. 3. As the story progresses, slip the Pharaoh's daughter figure, and then the Miriam figure between the folds of the bulrushes piece.

Another Idea: Use the Moses-in-the-basket figure from this page. Cut out the figure and cover it with clear Con-Tact paper. Place some plastic greenery, such as used in a fish tank, in a shallow pan or plastic container. Pour a little water in the stontainer. Let children put Moses in the bulrushes while you retell the story.

Sink or Float

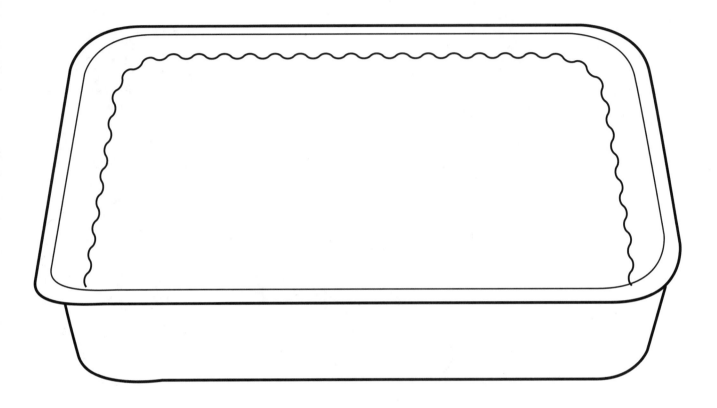

Materials: • garden planting tray or rectangle dish • water • various toys and items for the room

Directions: 1. Fill the tray or dish up with several inches of water. 2. Children search the room and choose waterproof item to test in the water. 3. Before taking a turn to put item in the water, each child guesses if their item will sink or float.

What to Say: Moses' mom painted something special on the basket to make sure it floated on the water. Let's see if your object will float on top of the water like Baby Moses' basket or sink.

Baby, Basket, Bulrushes

finished craft

Materials: • copies of this page enlarged by 150 percent, one for each child • different colors of construction paper • scissors
Directions: 1. Children trace their hand four times on sheets of construction paper. 2. Assist as children cut out paper hands. 3. Children glue the hands to the front of the basket to make them look like bulrushes.
What to Say: God used Miriam to help her brother be safe. We can use our hands to help God.

Where Is the Baby?

Materials: • copies of this page, one for each child • crayons
Directions: Children color the shapes with a tiny basket in them to find baby Moses in a big basket, then color the rest of the page.
What to Say: Baby Moses is in the bulrushes. Miriam is serving God by watching her brother. Can you find baby Moses?

Chapter 9
Moses Talks to Pharaoh

Memory Verse

[God is] more wonderful than all those
who are around him. Psalm 89:7

Story to Share

"Moses," God commanded. "Go to Pharaoh, the king of Egypt. Tell him that I want you to take my people, God's people, out of their slavery in Egypt."

Moses was worried! Pharaoh wanted huge monuments and statues made to look like him. And Pharaoh wanted the Israelite slaves to make them!

Moses did as God said. "You think your God can tell me what to do?" shouted Pharaoh. "Your people will work harder than ever!"

Pharaoh gave new orders to God's people: "You must not only make the bricks from mud and straw, but you must also gather the straw from the fields."

God was angry. It was time for Pharaoh and the Egyptians to be punished.

"What?" screamed Pharaoh one day. "What do you mean the rivers are red?"

Yes, the rivers were red. God had caused the streams and canals, ponds, and even the puddles to fill with blood. The fish swimming in the water died. Egypt smelled horrible!

Moses asked Pharaoh to let God's people go. "No," Pharaoh said again.

Next, God sent frogs everywhere—thousands of them! Frogs were on Pharaoh's throne, his bed, and even in his crown. Everywhere you heard, "Ribbet, ribbet!" But Pharaoh still would not let the people go.

God sent flies to buzz around the Egyptians' heads. Then he sent a disease on the cattle of the Egyptians. He sent hail and thunderstorms. He even sent locust insects, which ate every green leaf in Egypt. He covered the light from the sun for three days and all was dark, dark, dark. But did Pharaoh listen? No, he still would not respect God.

Pharaoh's disrespect meant the oldest son from every Egyptian household died. When Pharaoh's own son died, he knew it was because he hadn't listened to God and let God's people leave. He called Moses and his brother Aaron to the palace.

"Take your people and go," Pharaoh told Moses. God's people were free!

based on Exodus 7:1—10:29

Discussion Questions

1. Which of the bad things that happened in Egypt do you think was the worst?
2. Obeying is a way of showing respect. Who obeyed God—Pharaoh or Moses? Who disobeyed God—Pharaoh or Moses? Are you more like Pharaoh or Moses?

Pharaoh's Throne Room

Directions: 1. Children search picture for the items in the box and circle them when found. 2. Children color the picture.

What to Say: Pharaoh thought he was the most important person in the kingdom, but God is more wonderful than Pharaoh or anyone else!

More Wonderful

To the tune of "If You're Happy and You Know It."

God's more wonderful than the rest. Yes, he is!   ***stomp, stomp***
God's more wonderful than the rest. Yes, he is!   ***stomp, stomp***
He's more wonderful than the rest
For we know that he's the best.
Oh, God's more wonderful than the rest. Yes, he is!   ***stomp, stomp***

Materials: • gold or yellow copies of this page, one for each child plus one for sample   • scissors   • star pattern
• 9x12-inch felt sheets, one for each child   • dowel rods, one for each child   • stapler   • glue   • decorative tape
Preparation: Follow directions below to make a sample flag for children to reference.
Directions: 1. Children cut out and then glue the letters and the star on the felt. 2. Staple the felt to the dowel rod for each child. Cover the staples
with tape to avoid injury. 3. Sing the song to the tune of "If You're Happy and You Know It," waving flags and stomping feet on "Yes, he is!"

Wonderful God

_____

has a wonderful God.

_[God is] more wonderful than
all those who are around him._

Psalm 89:7

Materials: • copies of this page, one for each child • ink pad • crayons
**What to Say: Our God is wonderful! And he cares for us by giving us many wonderful things.
Let's use our thumbs to make drawings of some of our favorite things God has made.**
Directions: 1. Assist children to write their names on the blank line. 2. Help them to press thumbs in ink pad and then make thumbprints on paper.
3. Encourage children to use crayons to draw details on their thumbprints to make them into things that God has made (flowers, animals, people, etc.)

Run to God

The children of Israel knew who to run to for help. Was it to Pharaoh or to God? Follow the path of the frogs to end up in Pharaoh's throne room. Follow the stars to find Heaven—God's throne room.

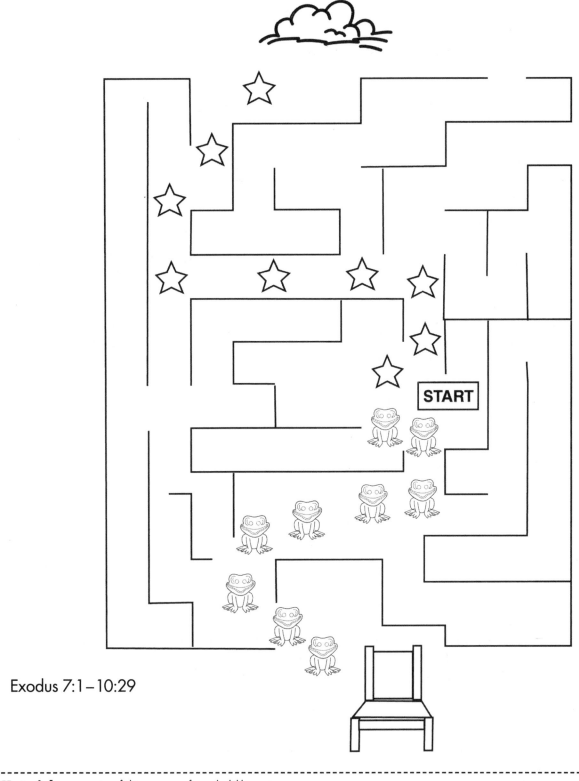

Exodus 7:1–10:29

Materials: • copies of this page, one for each child • crayons

Directions: Children color the picture.

What to Say: Do you ever get frightened? Maybe you are afraid of someone bigger than you are. Maybe you are afraid of storms.
(Children respond.) **Our God is stronger than anyone or anything around you. So when you are afraid, run to your wonderful God.**

Chapter 10
Moses and the Red Sea

 ## Memory Verse

The people of Israel went through the sea on dry ground. Exodus 14:22

Story to Share

God's people had been slaves for many years. Now God wanted His people to go free.

God sent ten plagues on the people of Egypt. God made these bad things happen so Pharaoh would know that God is in charge, not men—even Pharaoh.

When Pharaoh finally got tired of the plagues, he said, "Leave! Go!" He was afraid of what else God might do. So God's people left Egypt.

When Pharaoh heard that the people had gone, he changed his mind! He decided he didn't want them to leave. He had his army chase God's people to bring them back.

When Moses and God's people reached the Red Sea they could not cross. "Oh, no," the people said to Moses. "How are we going to cross the Red Sea?"

"Don't worry," Moses said. "God knows a way to keep us safe. God will take care of us."

Moses stretched out his hand over the Red Sea. The water separated and made a path in the middle of the sea. God sent a wind and made the ground dry.

God's people crossed the Red Sea on dry ground! Everyone was safe. God took good care of his people. Once they were through, God closed up the water on Pharaoh's army and stopped them from getting to God's people.

—based on Exodus 5:1–2; 12:31–32; 13:17—14:31

Discussion Questions

1. Have you ever been afraid? God will take care of you just like he took care of God's people.
2. How can you ask God to help you not be afraid? Pray.

Bible Story Book

Materials: • copies of this page and page 54, enlarge to 150 percent • scissors • two plastic or metal rings • hole punch

Directions: Cut out the four pictures on the solid lines. Punch two holes at the top of each page as indicated.
2. Place the scenes in order. 4. Place the rings through the holes to attach all of the pages together. 5. To tell story, hold the booklet so all the children can easily see the pictures. Flip the pages to the different scenes as you retell the Bible story. 6. Say often, God took care of his people.

Another Idea: Each child carries a stuffed animal or a backpack as you lead them on a walk around your classroom. Say, **Let's pretend we are leaving Egypt like God's people did. Let's walk a long way together. God took care of his people and he'll take care of us!**

Find a Way

Let My People Go

God said, "Let my people go."
Pharaoh said, "No, no, no."
God sent plagues—there were ten.
Pharaoh said, "Go! Don't do it again."

God's people packed up their stuff.
Then God said, "Go! That's enough."
They left Egypt very fast.
They were free—free at last.

They followed God's cloud in the day.
At night pillar of fire led the way.
The people traveled far and wide,
Until they stopped by the Red Sea's side.

"What will we do?" they began to say.
Moses said, "God will find a way."
God moved the water from the ground.
And they crossed the Red Sea, safe and sound.

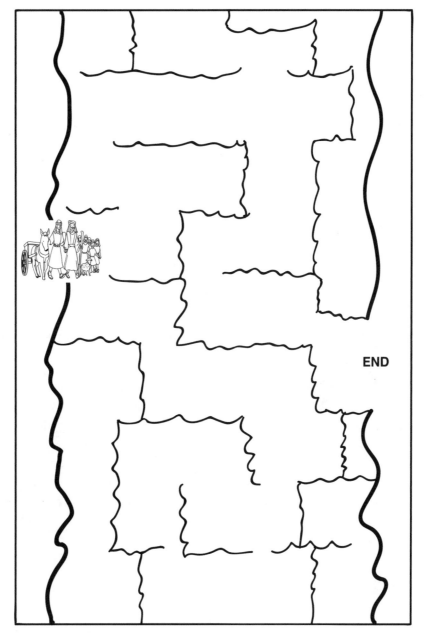

END

Materials: • copies of this page, one for each child • crayons
What to Say: Help the people find their way across the sea. Let's see which path goes all the way across the sea.
Directions: 1. Help the children find the correct path through the maze. 2. While the children color the picture read the poem to them.

Shape Sort

Materials: • copies of this page, one for each child • scissors • paper clips • crayons

Preparation: Cut out puzzle squares and the three shapes with figures, and then paper clip them together. Make one set for each child.

Directions: 1. Children color the puzzle and the figures. 2. Help the children match the three figures to the blank shapes on the puzzle.

What to Say: This is a picture of the people crossing the Red Sea. God took care of his people.

Chapter 11
Israelites in the Desert

Memory Verse

Do everything without complaining. Philippians 2:14

Story to Share

God's people were joyful when God helped Moses lead them from slavery in Egypt. They sang songs and danced, and they were thankful that they were safe.

God's people weren't sure which way to travel as they left Egypt. But God had a plan for them. He had a special place he wanted them to go. So he gave them a cloud by day and a pillar of fire at night to follow.

After traveling for about three days, God's people were tired and thirsty. They had been walking for three days without any water to drink. Then some people in the front of the crowd saw springs of water ahead of them. God's people were so excited!

But as they drew closer and actually tasted the water, they found it was bitter. They could not drink this water after all. Now God's people were disappointed.

"I'm so thirsty," said one.

"Moses, why did you bring us out into the desert to die of thirst?" another asked with anger. "You should have left us in Egypt."

Soon all the people could think about was their thirst and hunger. They grumbled about everything! They had forgotten completely about God's miracle of helping them leave slavery in Egypt. More importantly, they forgot God's promise that he would always care for them.

Moses prayed and asked God what he should do with all these grumbly people. God was not pleased with his people's grumbling, but he helped them anyway.

"Throw a piece of wood into the water, Moses," said God. "The water will turn sweet, and the people can drink it." Moses obeyed God and the water became sweet. God's people were happy as they drank it.

Moses told the people, "God does not like to hear grumbling. He will always take care of us."

—*based on Exodus 15:22–27*

Discussion Questions

1. Why were God's people grumbling?
2. What do you grumble about? What does God think of grumbling?

Picture This

Garden of Smiles

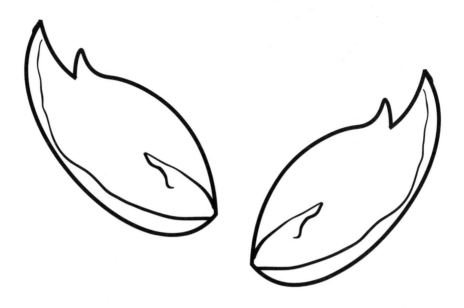

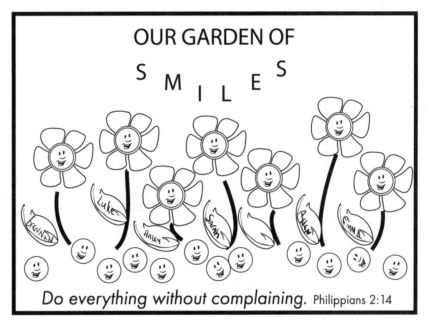

Materials: • copies of this page and page 60 • card stock, white, green and yellow • scissors • green construction paper • blue butcher paper • marker • paint brushes • glue • colored cereals

Preparation: Copy the leaves on this page to green card stock, the flower from page 60 to white card stock, and the smiley face from page 60 to yellow card stock, making one set for each child. Cut out all pieces. Make extra copies of the smiley faces. Lay a blue piece of butcher on a table. Write the Bible verse on the bottom. Write "Our Garden of Smiles" along the top of the board. Cut green construction paper into slightly curved strips of varying lengths, making one for each child.

Continued on next page . . .

Continued from previous page.

Directions: 1. Give each child a paint brush and glue. Children brush glue on one petal of their flowers, then sprinkle it with cereal. Continue with each petal. 2. Print the name of each child on their leaf. 3. Children glue their smiles to the middles of their flowers. 4. Assist children as they glue green construction paper strips on poster (for stems), and then attach their flowers and leaves to a stem. Make sure to vary the heights. 5. Glue extra smiles along the bottom of the picture.

Book of Blessings

Thank You
God
for

finished craft

Materials: • card-stock copies of this page, one for each child • paper copies of this page, two for each child • scissors • transparent tape • stickers (of food, animals, hearts, toys, etc.) • crayons

Preparation: Cut out the patterns. For the paper copies, cut across the dotted line and discard the top halves of the copies. Tape the first bottom half on the right side of the card-stock piece. Tape a second piece on the left side.

Directions: 1. Children color the pictures in their books, finishing the faces to look like themselves.
2. Assist the children in choosing stickers for the things for which they want to thank God.

What to Say: Ask each child to close their book. Pray, **We thank you, God, for all the joy you give to us. We thank you for . . .**
One at a time, each child says what is on the first page of their book. **We thank you for all these blessings and many more. Amen.**

Chapter 12
The Ten Commandments

 ## Memory Verse

LORD . . . teach me your laws. Psalm 119:108

Story to Share

While God's people were camping at Mt. Sinai, God gave them ten special laws to help them know how to live and worship him better. God gave these rules to Moses to share with his people. These laws are recorded in the Bible. God still wants us to follow them today.

Four of the rules were about God. We should worship God only—the one true God. We shouldn't bow down to idols, or love anything or anyone more than we love God. God doesn't want us to make fun of his name or say it in anger. God wants us to spend one day every week in rest and worship. God said, "Remember the Sabbath day, and keep it holy."

Then God told Moses to teach the people to honor their parents. He does not want us to disobey or disrespect our parents.

"Don't take the lives of others," God then said. "And if you are married, keep your wedding vows."

God also gave us the laws that say "Don't take what isn't yours" and "Don't lie or deceive anyone." The tenth law God gave was "Don't wish you could have something that belongs to someone else. Be happy with your own belongings."

God gave us ten rules to live by. These are ten rules we can learn to help us worship God better.

—based on Exodus 20

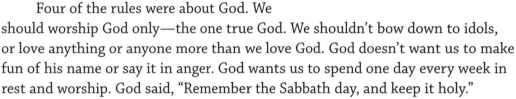 ## Discussion Questions

1. **How many rules did God give Moses to help us worship and live right?** (Ten.)

2. **How can we learn God's laws?** (Listening in church, asking family members to read from the Bible.)

What Goes Together?

Materials: • copies of this page, one for each child • crayons

Directions: Children how to draw a line between the paths to connect the things that go together.

What to Say: Buildings and people looked different in Bible days. Even their Bible looked different from ours today. One thing remains the same—we must learn about God.

About God

Materials: • copies of this page, one for each child • banana slices • blue gelatin powder • paper plates • crayons • scissors
Preparation: For each child, prepare a paper plate with banana slices and some gelatin powder.
What to Say: Today we're going to learn something fun! Dip your yellow bananas into the blue gelatin powder. Does anyone know the powder's new color? (Green) We just learned that when you mix something yellow with something blue you get something green. Jesus wants us to learn about God, too. Hold up pictures. You can learn that God created the earth, that Jesus died for our sins, and that Jesus loves everyone.
Directions: 1. Children color their papers. 2. Assist children to cut out the cards..

I Can!

LORD . . . teach me your laws.
Psalm 119:108

I can learn about God.

Materials: • copies of this page, one for each child   • crayons

What to Say: Who is teaching us about God in this picture?

Directions: 1. Children color the pictures. 2. Read aloud "I can learn about God," as children trace the letters. Say the sentence aloud with children.

Right Rules

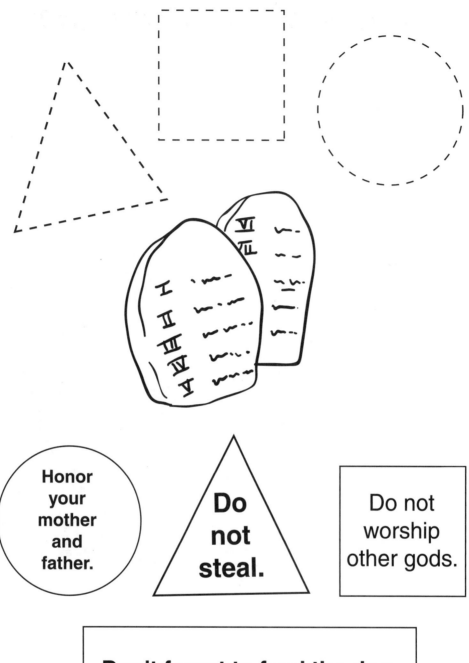

Honor your mother and father.

Do not steal.

Do not worship other gods.

Don't forget to feed the dog.

Materials: • copies of this page, one for each child • crayons • scissors • glue

Directions: 1. Children color and then cut out the shapes. 2. Read the sentences in the shapes. Ask the children which shape's sentence is not a law God gave Moses. 3. Children glue the shapes that are laws from God to the matching dashed-line shapes.

What to Say: God wanted Moses and his people to learn about him. When you learn God's law to honor your father and mother, you will obey when they tell you to feed the dog. When you learn God doesn't want you to steal, you won't take a toy that doesn't belong to you. Learning about God helps you do what is right.

Chapter 13

Daniel in the Lion's Den

 ## Memory Verse

My God sent his angel. Daniel 6:22

Daniel was a man that loved God. Daniel had been in Babylon a long time. He was able to help the kings of Babylon understand confusing things because God told Daniel the answers.

This amazed the kings and they made Daniel a leader over their land. When King Darius' became king, he put Daniel in charge of the kingdom. But other people didn't want Daniel to rule over them. So they planned to make the king angry at Daniel!

"King Darius," they said. "You are so wonderful. Nobody should pray to anyone but you. If anyone breaks that rule, they should be thrown into the den of lions."

King Darius thought that was a great idea. But Daniel still prayed to God three times a day. When the men saw Daniel praying, they went to the king. "Daniel is breaking your rule!" they said. The king was sorry he had made the rule. He loved Daniel. Now he had to throw Daniel in the lions' den.

Early the next morning, the king rushed to the lions' den. "Daniel!" he called. "Has your God rescued you from the lions?"

"Yes!" Daniel said. "My God sent an angel to shut the lions' mouths. They haven't hurt me at all." He was protected by God.

King Darius was very happy. He had his men take Daniel out of the lions' den. King Darius wrote to all the people and said, "I order people everywhere to respect and obey Daniel's God. He is the living God."

Daniel kept working for King Darius and was happy.

—*Daniel 6*

Discussion Questions
1. Where did the king put Daniel when he broke the rule?
2. Why didn't the lions hurt Daniel?

Daniel Bible Story Figures

Materials: • copies of this page and page 69, one of each for each child • crayons • scissors • resealable plastic bag
Directions: 1. Children color pictures. 2. Help them cut out the figures. 3. Retell the Bible story as children use their figures to act it out. 4. Children place figures in a resealable plastic bag so they can take them home and tell the Bible story to someone else.

Daniel Dot-to-Dot

Materials: • copies of this page, one for each child • crayons

Directions: Help the children complete the dot-to-dot picture of Daniel in each scene.

What to Say: Where is Daniel in the scene at the top of your page? What is Daniel doing? Yes, he's praying to God. Where is Daniel in the scene at the bottom of the page? What is Daniel doing. Wherever he was, Daniel prayed to God. God took care of Daniel.

Lion Puppet

Materials: • copies of this page, one for each child • crayons

Directions: 1. Children color the picture. 2. Help children fold the page on the dashed lines, accordion style.

3. Show children how to hold the picture from the back to make the lion's mouth open and close.

What to Say: God shut the lions' mouths so they couldn't hurt Daniel. God took care of Daniel and he'll take care of you!

Chapter 14
David and Goliath

Memory Verse

I'm coming against you in the name of the LORD. 1 Samuel 17:45

Story to Share

God's army gathered together to battle the Philistines. One of the Philistines was a giant called Goliath.

Goliath shouted at God's army and said, "Choose one of your men and have him face me. If he is able to defeat me, we will become your slaves." All of God's soldiers were afraid of Goliath.

David was the youngest son in a family. His three brothers were in God's army. One day, David took some food for his brothers in the army camp. Goliath came out again and God's soldiers ran.

"I will go battle him myself. God will take care of me," David said.

David stood up to Goliath and told him, "I am fighting you in the name of the Lord. This very day God will help me win."

David put one stone into his sling and slung it at Goliath. The stone hit Goliath right in the forehead. The giant fell down. So David won the fight against Goliath with a sling and a stone.

God amazed his army with a little stone that knocked down a giant.

—*based on 1 Samuel 17*

Discussion Questions

1. Why was God's army afraid of Goliath? He was a giant, bigger than any of them.
2. Why was David brave enough to fight the giant?
3. Are there things that scare you? Is God big enough to help you with them?

Pouch and Sling

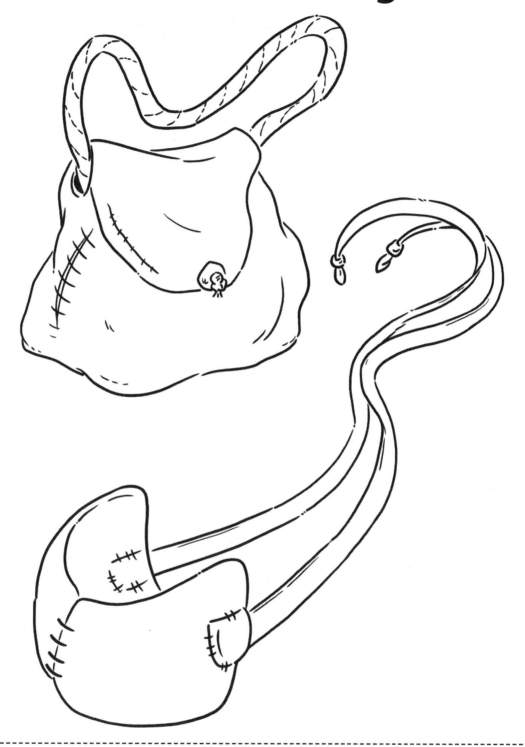

Materials: • copy of this page and page 74 • crayons or markers • scissors • butcher paper • five small stones
Preparation: Color both copied pages. Cut out the sling and pouch. On butcher paper, draw a very tall human figure to represent Goliath. Trace a smaller figure to be Daniel. Post figures on a wall.
What to Say: **The army of God's people were very afraid of Goliath.** Point to the large shape of Goliath on your wall. **No one wanted to fight him!** Hold up your colored copy of page 74. **But there was one young shepherd boy who trusted God and wasn't afraid!**
Directions: 1. Hold up the pouch and sling and the five little stones. Children help you count the stones. 2. Pretend to put one stone in the sling and hit Goliath in the forehead. 3. Pull the Goliath figure off the wall and let it fall to the floor.
More Ideas: Use a carpeted area or cover the floor with blankets. Get a measuring tape or some yard sticks. Children take turns lying down in a long line, head-to-toe. Measure the children to show how many children it would take to make a giant nine feet tall.

Knock Down the Giant

Materials: • brightly colored copies of this page and page 76 • scissors • transparent tape or glue • large Styrofoam tray or platter
• 9x12-inch cake pan • dried beans or rice • bean bags • newspaper or towel

Preparation: Cut out the head and body of Goliath. Tape or glue the two "giant" sections onto the Styrofoam tray. Fill the cake pan
with dried beans or rice and place "giant" tray so that it is standing up in the cake pan. Place on one side of the playing area.

Directions: 1. Children take turns tossing beanbags at the giant. 2. When the giant is knocked over, children say the memory verse, "I'm
coming against you in the name of the Lord" (1 Samuel 17:45). 3. Place "giant" tray upright and play again as time and interest allow.

Chapter 15
David the Shepherd Boy

 Memory Verse

Always be joyful. 1 Thessalonians 5:16

Story to Share

David was a shepherd boy. He took his father's sheep to the hills around Bethlehem and watched over them. David watched the sheep on sunny days and rainy days, too.

Being a shepherd was a lonely life. And sometimes it was scary, too. One day David heard, "Baaa, baaa." It sounded like a lamb was saying, "Help me, help me." When David turned around he saw a bear carrying a lamb in his teeth.

"Stop," shouted David. He quickly put a smooth stone in his sling and whirled it around his head. As he let go of one end of the sling, the stone flew through the air and hit the bear.

David ran toward the stunned bear and grabbed the lamb out of the bear's mouth. Furious, the bear ran toward David. "Help me, Father God," David must have prayed. He grabbed the bear, hit it, and watched as the bear fell to the ground. It was dead! "Thank you, God, thank you," David said.

Even when David was afraid or lonely, he knew God was with him. He wrote many songs to sing to God. One day when all of the lambs were lying quietly on the green grass, David played his harp and sang, "The LORD is my shepherd. He gives me everything I need" (Psalm 23:1).

David was a happy shepherd boy. He was God's child.

—*based on Psalm 23*

Discussion Questions

1. Do you like to sing while you are playing? Do you sing because you are happy?
2. Do you think your family is happy when you are happy?

Color by Number

Key: 1 = | Brown | 2 = | Blue | 3 = | Green | 4 = | Yellow |

Materials: • copies of this page, one for each child   • crayons
Preparation: For each copy, color in the Key so children can more easily follow the instructions.
What to Say: Color the picture according to the numbers in each shape. For number 1, color brown; number 2, blue; number 3, green; number 4, yellow.
Directions: Children color pages.

Sewing Lambs

Materials: • poster-board copies of this page, one for every two children • scissors • hole punch
• yarn • transparent tape • black crayons **Optional** • clear Con-Tact paper

Preparation: Cut out lambs. Punch holes where indicated on the lambs. Cut the yarn into 24-inch lengths, making one for
each child. Wrap tape around one end of each yarn length. Tie one the other end of the yarn to a hole in the lamb.

Directions: 1. Children color the face and legs of the lambs black. 3. Assist children in "sewing" the yarn around the lamb.

Optional: For a longer-lasting sewing card, cover each lamb with clear Con-Tact paper before cutting out and punching holes.

Happy Lambs

Snowflake wants to help me be happy all week. Will you help me glue a cotton ball to my lamb each day I am happy? The Bible says to "Be joyful always." I want to be God's happy child.

XOXO,

Materials: • copies of this page, one for each child • scissors • resealable plastic sandwich bags • cotton balls

Directions: 1. Children cut out the lambs and notes. 2. Assist children in writing their names to sign the notes. 3. Children glue notes to the back of their lambs. 4. Children place lambs in plastic bags. 5. Children count out seven cotton balls and place them in their plastic bags.

What to Say: You can take your lamb home with these cotton balls. His name is Snowflake. Every day that you remember to be happy, glue a cotton ball to Snowflake. Snowflake will be happy, too, when he has his wool to keep him warm.

Lamb Masks

Materials: • card-stock copies of this page, one for each child • scissors • black crayons • glue • cotton balls • craft sticks • transparent tape

Preparation: Cut out a lamb mask and eye holes for each child.

Directions: 1. Children color the sheep faces black. 2. Children glue cotton balls around the face on the masks. 3. Help children to tape a craft stick handle to their masks. 4. Lead the children in "bleating" the verse: "Aaaalwaaays beeee joooyfuuuul." (1 Thessalonians 5:16).

Chapter 16
David Forgives King Saul

Forgive, and you will be forgiven. Luke 6:37

Story to Share

Saul was king when David killed Goliath. Saul was happy to win the battle. When King Saul returned home, the women were singing and dancing.

"King Saul has killed his thousands," the women sang, "But David has killed his ten thousands." From that day on, King Saul was angry and jealous of David. He was afraid David would take the kingdom away from him.

David had to hide from King Saul. So he took some of his men and they hid in caves and forests.

One day, David heard that King Saul and his army were looking for him. He hid deep in a cave.

As David waited, he saw that King Saul had grown tired and was lying on the ground near the entrance of the cave. There were no soldiers near him.

"Hurry," whispered one of David's men. "Here's your chance to kill him."

But David knew God would not be pleased if he was mean back at King Saul. Instead David just snuck up behind King Saul and carefully cut off a piece of King Saul's robe.

When King Saul awoke and left the cave, David secretly followed him. King Saul was carefully walking among the rocks on the hillside. David stood high above him and called, "King Saul!"

King Saul spun around in surprise. He watched as David bowed in respect. "Is that you, David?" the king asked.

"Yes," answered David. "Today I was close enough to kill you, but I couldn't kill the Lord's chosen king. I have chosen to forgive you instead."

King Saul never admitted his jealousy toward David. But David had chosen forgiveness and did not harm.

—*based on 1 Samuel 24*

Discussion Questions

1. Did David do anything wrong to Saul to make him angry?
2. Can you forgive a friend who is angry with you?

Saul and David

Materials: • copies of this page, one for each child • scissors • fabric scraps • crayons • glue • transparent tape
Preparation: Cut fabric scraps into 2x4-inch pieces.
Directions: 1. Children color their pages. 2. Assist children to glue the fabric robe to King Saul. 3. Help children cut a piece off Saul's robe and tape to David's hand. 4. Retell the story as children use the figures to act it out.

Puzzle Pieces

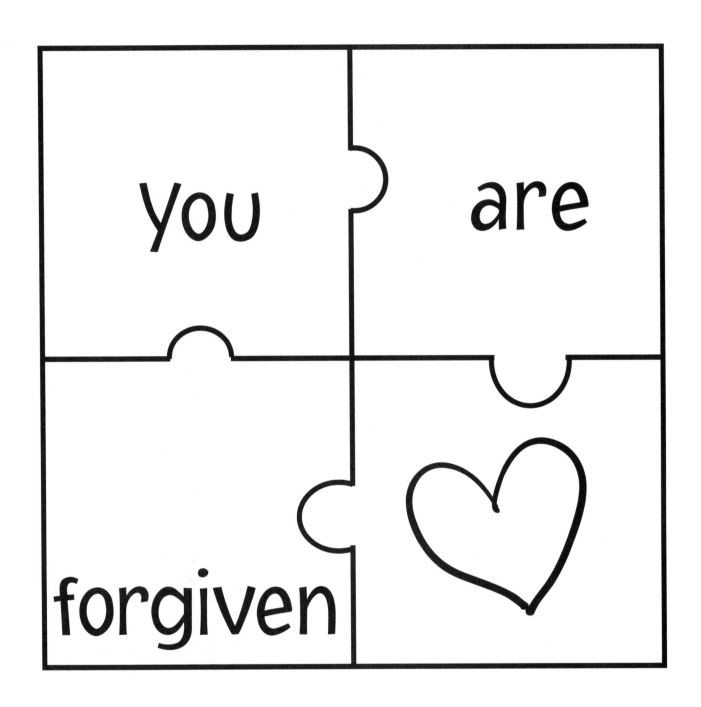

Materials: • colored copies of this page, one for every four children (each puzzle a different color)
• clear Con-Tact paper • scissors • paper bag or basket
Preparation: Cover each puzzle with clear Con-Tact paper. Cut apart all the pieces and put pieces in a paper bag or basket.
Directions: 1. Each child chooses a piece. 2. At your signal, children with the same color puzzle piece come together to put their puzzles together. When each team completes the puzzle, team members announce, "You are forgiven!"

Shapes of Forgiveness

Materials: • copies of this page and page 86, one of each for each child • crayons • scissors • glue
Directions: 1. Children color the pages and cut out Saul, David, and sun shapes.
2. Children find the cutout that fits each empty shape on page 86 and glue it in place.
What to Say: It doesn't matter if the person who hurt us is big or little, God still wants us to forgive.
Say this with me, "Big or little, I will forgive. That's the way God wants us to live."

Chapter 17
Jonah

 Memory Verse

Jonah prayed to the LORD his God. Jonah 2:1

Story to Share

Jonah was a man who told lots of people about God. God told Jonah he must go to a city called Nineveh. But Jonah didn't want to go there. So instead, Jonah ran away! He got on a ship that was sailing far away.

But God already knew where Jonah was. He sent a big storm. The water came up over the sides of the ship. "We're going to crash!" yelled the men on the ship. Jonah was sound asleep in the bottom of the ship. The men woke him up and asked, "Why is this happening to us?"

Jonah knew why God sent the storm. "I ran away from God," he told the other men. "You need to throw me into the sea. Then God will take away the storm." They didn't want to throw him overboard so they tried everything they could to try to sail back to the land. The storm only got worse.

The men picked up Jonah and threw him into the sea. The storm stopped. God sent a big fish to swallow Jonah. Jonah was safe inside the fish for three days and three nights.

Jonah prayed and told God he was sorry. Jonah told God he would do what God asked him to do. He would go where God wanted him to go. Then the fish spat Jonah out, right on the shore. He was safe. God took care of Jonah.

Jonah went and told the people of Nineveh to stop being bad or God would punish them. They all stopped and starting doing what was right because Jonah obeyed God.

—based on Jonah 1:1—2:10

Discussion Questions

1. Why did Jonah not want to tell the people of Nineveh about God?
2. Should we always obey God's Word?
3. Where do we find God's Word?

Jonah's Journey

Materials: • copies of this page, one for each child and one extra • scissors • ribbon • crayons • glue • construction paper
• scissors • ribbon • crayons • transparent tape

Preparation: Prepare a sample following directions below. Cut a 12-inch length of ribbon for each child.

Directions: 1. Children color the paper and glue to a piece of construction paper for sturdiness. 2. Children cut out the scene and Jonah figure. 3. Assist children as they tape a 12-inch length of ribbon to the top of the scene where there is a line, and then tape the Jonah figure to the other end of the ribbon. 4. Retell the Bible story, holding the sample you prepared so that all the children can see and imitate the way you move Jonah to act out the story.

Jonah Ran Away

Materials: • copies of this page, one for each child • crayons • fish stickers
Directions: 1. Help the children follow Jonah's path to the boat, the fish, and finally to Nineveh. 2. Read the story again on page 87 while the children color their maze. 3. Children place fish stickers near the big fish and the boat.

Jonah Story Book

God told the fish
to put Jonah on
the shore. God
took care of Jonah.

Jonah prayed
inside the fish.

I can pray to God.
God takes care of me.

Jonah
Prayed

Materials: • copies of this page, one for each child • scissors • crayons

Directions: 1. Children cut out the folding book. 2. Help the children fold their pages on the folding lines to make the book. 3. While the children color their books, read the pages to them.

What to Say: Jonah prayed when he was inside the fish. God took care of Jonah and had the fish put him on land. We can pray to God, too. God will take care of us, too.

Where Is Jonah?

Materials: • copies of this page, one for each child • scissors • transparent tape • crayons
Preparation: Cut out the two fish sections for each child.
Directions: 1. Help children tape the two fish sections together at the top. 2. Show how to look inside and find Jonah. Read the verse to the children.
What to Say: Today's Bible words are "Jonah prayed to . . . God." Ask children to repeat the words after you. **God kept Jonah safe inside the fish for three days and three nights. Then God had the fish put Jonah safely on the shore. God took care of Jonah.**

Chapter 18
God Is with Joseph

 ## Memory Verse

Guard what God has trusted you with. 1 Timothy 6:20

 ## Story to Share

Joseph was a boy who had eleven brothers. He was the youngest. His father, Jacob, loved him very much. He gave him a colorful coat.

Joseph's brothers were angry Joseph was so loved. The brothers took Joseph's coat and sold Joseph to traders who were traveling to faraway lands. The traders took Joseph to Egypt, where he became a slave.

One day, the slave master's wife told a terrible lie about Joseph. The master believed his wife, and Joseph was put in prison. Even though Joseph did not like being in prison, he asked God to help him be cheerful. Knowing God was with him—even in prison—made Joseph's heart happy.

It didn't take the jailer long to notice how happy Joseph was. He saw how Joseph sang to calm a tired prisoner. He also saw how Joseph gave some of his food to another prisoner who was hungry. The jailer knew Joseph could be trusted.

"Joseph," the jailer said, "I am going to make you head of the prison."

Joseph was happy for the job the jailer gave him. He worked hard to take care of the prisoners. Each morning, he took water and cloths to the prisoners so they could wash.

When the prisoners asked how he could be so happy, Joseph told them, "My God is with me."

Joseph was faithful to God and did his job well. So God worked through Joseph to explain people's dreams to them.

When the king of Egypt had a dream he couldn't figure out, he called Joseph. Joseph explained Pharaoh's dream. The Pharaoh was so thankful to Joseph that he made him a great leader in Egypt.

God was happy with Joseph because he did his work well. God wants us to do our jobs well, too.

—*based on Genesis 37–41*

Discussion Questions

1. **How was Joseph able to be happy even though he had to work hard?**
2. **What kinds of jobs or chores do you have?** (Pick up toys, feed pets, set the table, etc.)
3. **How does God want you to behave when you do them?**

Stained Glass Coat

Materials: • colored card-stock copies of this page, one for every two children • scissors • washable markers
• coffee filters • clear Con-Tact paper • crayons • ribbon or yarn • spray bottle with water

Preparation: Cut out coat patterns. Cut ribbon or yarn into 8-inch lengths, making one for each child.

Directions: 1. Each child colors a coffee filter with markers. 2. Assist children to cover colored filter with clear Con-Tact paper. 3. Using a coat pattern, children trace the shape onto their coffee filter with a crayon and cut out. 4. Punch a hole at the top of each coat. 5. Assist children to thread a length of ribbon or yarn through the hole and tie in a loop for hanging. 6. Children spray the filters with water to make the colors bleed and then set aside to dry.

What to Say: Even though Joseph lost his beautiful coat, he was determined to behave the way that God wanted. When Joseph was in prison, he was the best prisoner he could be. When Joseph became a leader in Egypt, he was the best leader he could be. Joseph wanted to make God happy. We can give our lives to make God happy, too.

Joseph's Wardrobe

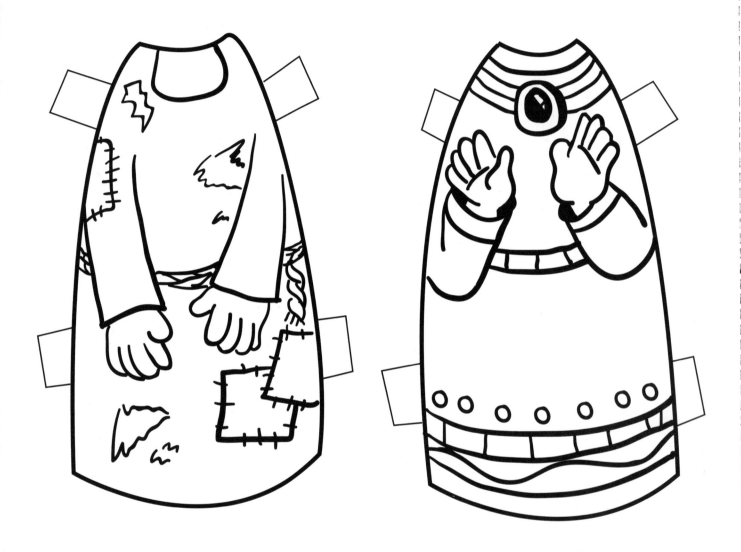

Materials: • copies of this page and page 95, one for each child   • scissors   • crayons   • gold glitter glue

Preparation: Cut out a Joseph and a set of clothes for each child.

Directions: 1. Children color Joseph and his clothes. 2. Assist the children in adding glue glitter to Joseph's Egyptian robe.
3. Retell the Bible story while children use Joseph figure and his clothes to act it out.

Chore Chart

_____'s Chore Chart	
Guard what God has trusted you with. 1 Timothy 6:20	

Sunday	Monday	Tuesday	Wednesday	Thursday	Friday	Saturday

Materials: • copies of this page, one for each child • crayons • scissors • resealable snack-sized plastic bags • stickers

Directions: 1. Children color and cut out the chore chart. 2. Send home the chore chart and a selection of small stickers in the plastic bags.

What to Say: Use your chart to remember to be responsible. After doing your chores each day pick your favorite sticker and place it on the chart. What are some chores you are asked to help with? How can you do your best job for God?

Chapter 19
Joseph

Memory Verse

Love is kind. 1 Corinthians 13:4

Story to Share

When Joseph was a young boy, his brothers sold him to people who took him far away to Egypt. Even though Joseph ended up far from home, God was with him. God protected him and helped Joseph become an important person in Egypt. God gave Joseph answers to the king's questions. The king made Joseph a very important leader in Egypt.

God told Joseph that there would be a famine. A famine is a long time when no food grows. So the king told Joseph to help store up food so they would be ready when that happened. When the food stopped growing, Egypt still had food. Joseph was in charge of giving it to the needy.

Joseph's brothers became hungry. "Let's go to Egypt and get some food," they said. So they headed to Egypt to bring back food. The brothers didn't know Joseph was a very powerful man in Egypt. Joseph would be the one to give them the food they wanted.

Joseph had been in Egypt a long time. He had grown older and looked different than when he was a little boy. When he saw his brothers for the first time in so long he was upset. He had missed his family so much. He could have stayed angry at them for the bad thing they had done to him when he was a boy. Joseph could have refused to give them food or even ordered them to be killed.

Instead, Joseph gave them food for their entire family. He sent for the family to come and live in Egypt so they would have plenty of food during the famine. God used the bad thing the brothers did to allow Joseph to help them and many other people. God wants us to be forgiving and kind.

—based on Genesis 43:29

Discussion Questions

1. What words are easy for you to say? Kind words? Angry words?
2. Which words please Jesus?
3. Is there someone you are angry with that you should forgive?

Joseph's Memory Verse

Love is kind. 1 Corinthians 13:4

finished craft

Materials: • copies of this page, one for each child • scissors • white paper lunch bags • crayons • glue
Preparation: Cut out a face and mouth for each child.
Directions: 1. Children color the pattern pieces and a white paper lunch bags to make a "coat of many colors."
2. Show the children how to glue the parts to the sack to make a puppet (see sketch).
What to Say: Listen to our memory verse: "Love is kind." Let's make puppet say that to the friend sitting next to us!

Catch a Smile

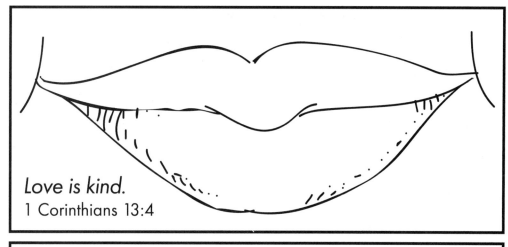

Love is kind.
1 Corinthians 13:4

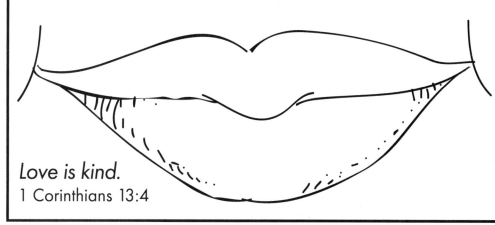

Love is kind.
1 Corinthians 13:4

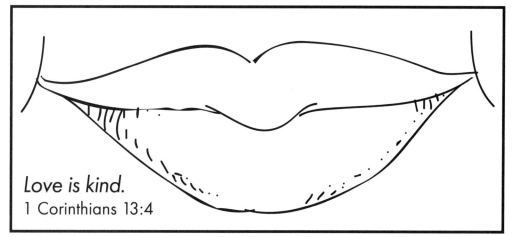

Love is kind.
1 Corinthians 13:4

Materials: • copies of this page, one for every three children • scissors • red and pink crayons • string • large magnet • paper clips
Preparation: Cut out smiles. Tie 3 inches of string to the large magnet.
Directions: 1. Children color smiles. 2. Slip a paper clip onto each smile and lay them on the floor. 3. Children take turns to use magnet to fish for and "catch" a smile.
What to Say: Want to know one way to catch a smile? Be kind. When you hold the door for people, they say, "Thank you" and smile. When you say, "Excuse me" and move out of a friend's way, they will likely say, "Thank you" and smile. But when you shove a friend, or grab toys out of another's hands, what happens? Instead of catching a smile, you catch a frown. Smiles are better!

Quiet Kindness

Love is kind. 1 Corinthians 13:4

Materials: • copies of this page, one for each child • crayons

Preparation: Make a picture of something you did during the week. Be the first to hold up the picture and talk about it. This will make it easier for the children to understand the activity.

Directions: 1. Children draw something with crayons that they did during the past week. They may also color the frames. 2. Allow time for the children to stand, hold up their picture, and share what they drew.

What to Say: Being kind means you are quiet while others are talking. But you may nod your head while your friends are talking, and when they are through say, "That was very interesting."

Kindness Hearts

1 Corinthians 13:4

Materials: • copy of this page, one for each child • crayons
Directions: Children trace the hearts, and color hearts and letters.
What to Say: I will say the verse aloud while you are coloring it, then we will say
it together. Who showed kindness in our Bible lesson today?

Chapter 20
Josiah

 ## Memory Verse

True worshipers will worship the Father. John 4:23

 ## Story to Share

Josiah was only eight years old when he was made king. When King Josiah was sixteen, he began to worship God. King Josiah loved God and obeyed his ways completely.

Josiah had noticed that many of his people had begun to worship idols. Idols were objects that people would pray to like they were gods. But Josiah wanted his whole kingdom to worship God only. For six years, Josiah worked to get rid of the idols. He had the altars used to worship idols torn down, and the idols ground into dust.

Because so many people were worshiping idols, God's temple, holy place—like a church, was not cared for properly. When King Solomon had built the temple, he had richly decorated the building to honor God. The walls and floors had been lined with carved cedar wood and gold. Even the doors and door posts had been beautifully carved. But it had been 250 years since repairs were made to the special temple.

Josiah was only twenty-six years old, but he knew it was important to have a place to worship God. He gave orders for the temple to be repaired.

Money was collected to buy the materials needed for the repairs. The men chosen to work on the temple were honest and could be trusted to work hard. They bought wood and stone to make repairs. When the temple was repaired, Josiah brought back the singers and musicians to celebrate.

God was pleased with the young king. He wants his house to be clean and in good repair. Josiah led the people in making a new vow of love and loyalty to the true God of Israel.

—based on 2 Kings 22:1–6

Discussion Questions

1. **How old was King Josiah when he gave orders for the temple to be cleaned?** (Twenty-six years old.)
2. **Who is old enough to help keep the church clean?** (Everyone.)

Path Sewing Card

the

Father.

John 4:23

worship

Church is fun!

will

worshipers

True

Materials: • card-stock copies of this page, one for each child • scissors • crayons • yarn • transparent tape • hole punch

Preparation: Cut out one card for each child. Punch a hole in the child and in every footprint. Cut yarn into 20-inch lengths. Wrap tape around one end of each yarn length to make it stiff and tie a knot at the opposite end.

Directions: 1. Children color their sewing cards. 2. Show how to lace the yarn through the hole by the child on the card and tape the knot to the back of the card. 3. Demonstrate how to "sew" the card to get the child to church. 4. Do this activity as a class, repeating the word of each footprint until you arrive at the church.

Clean Church Worksheet

Materials: • copies of this page, one for each child   • crayons

Directions: 1. Children circle or color the items that can be used to keep the church clean. 2. Say the finger play (below) with the children.

What to Say: I may be very little, (Point to self.) **and my muscles kinda small.** (Flex muscles.) **But I can use my hands** (Hold out hands.) **and feet,** (Point to feet.) **to keep my church** (Lace fingers with pointer fingers forming steeple.) **clean and neat.**

Build a Church

Materials: • copies of this page and page 106, one of each page for each child • scissors • crayons • glue • construction paper

Preparation: Cut out a set of church pieces for each child.

Directions: 1 Children color their church pieces. 2. Show how to glue the pieces to the construction paper to form a church. 3. Children draw a scene (sun, birds, trees, flowers, etc.) around the church.

What to Say: The people in Bible times called their place of worship a *temple*. What do we call our place of worship? (Church)

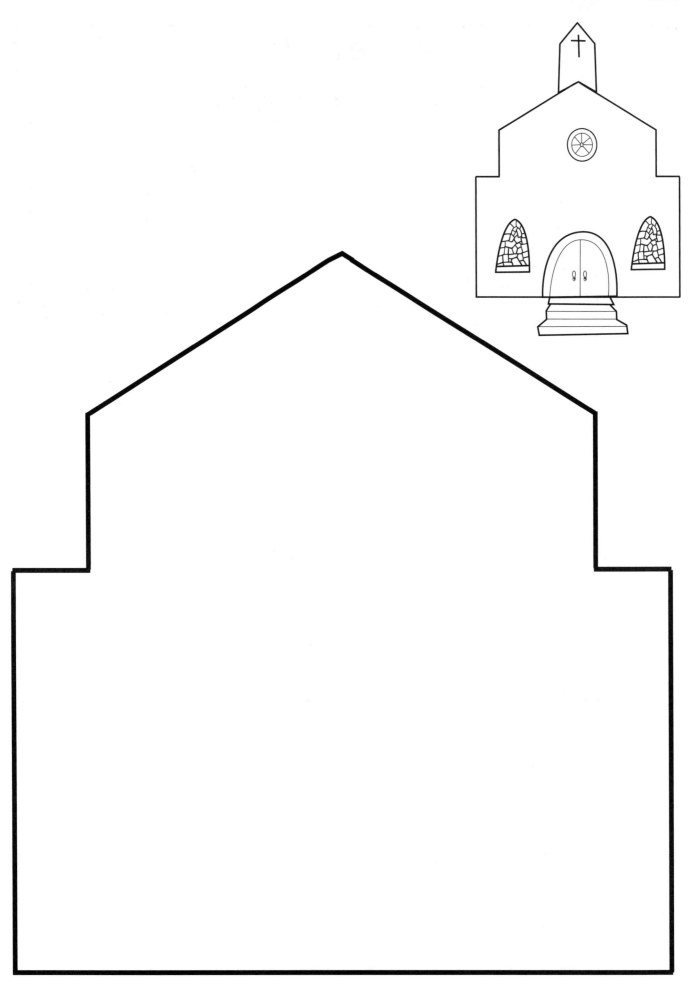

Chapter 21
Elijah and Elisha

 **Memory Verse**

Love one another. 1 Thessalonians 4:9

 Story to Share

Elijah was God's prophet. He knew that he would go to Heaven one day and would need someone to take his place. "God," he prayed. "Who shall I choose to take my place?"

"Go find Elisha," God told him. "He will take your place as prophet."

Elijah found Elisha in the field. He had twelve yoke of oxen pulling his plow. When Elijah got close to Elisha, he took his own cloak and threw it over Elisha's shoulders.

Elisha bowed his head. He loved Elijah and was honored to take his place. "I don't feel worthy," he whispered. With the prophet's cloak around his shoulders, he left his plow and followed Elijah to become a prophet.

One day after Elijah had gone to Heaven, Elisha went to Shunem. While he was there he met a rich man and woman. "Come, eat with us," they invited.

Elisha went to their home. "Thank you," he said after eating the delicious fruits and other good food. "The meal was so good."

"Come anytime," the couple urged. "We have an extra room just for you."

They gave Elisha his own room on the cool roof. The room had a bed, a stool, a table, and a lamp. It was a special place for Elisha to rest.

"This Shunemite couple is so loving," said Elisha. "I wish I knew what I could do to show my love for them."

"I know," a friend told Elisha. "This lady would like to have a son."

Elisha told the woman, "You shall have a son." God gave them a son.

What a joy the son was to the Shunemite woman. She and her husband loved a prophet of God. In return, Elisha was loving to them. They were God's children.

—*based on 2 Kings 4:8–17*

?? Discussion Questions

1. Do you think being loving encourages others to show love to you?
2. The Shunemite couple showed love to Elisha. Was he loving in return?
3. How can you show love to those who have shown love to you?

What's Wrong with Elisha's Room?

What's wrong with Elisha's room? In the picture below, there are five things that would have been strange to find in Elisha's room. Circle the strange sights, then color the picture.

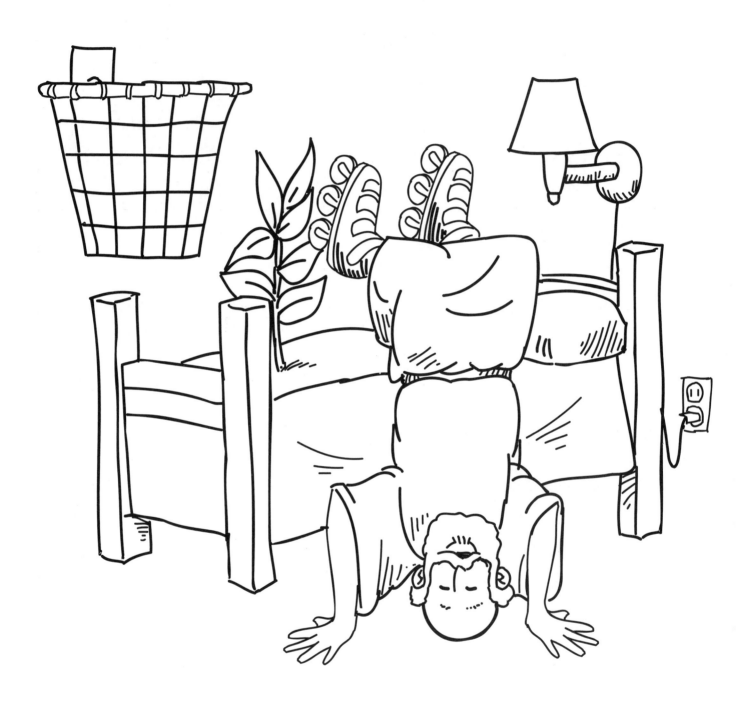

Materials: • copies of this page, one for each child   • crayons

Directions: 1. Children complete puzzle. 2. After the children have finished, discuss each thing that is wrong in the picture.

What to Say: Did the Shunemite couple have strange things in Elisha's room? No, they wanted everything to be perfect for the one they loved. They did their best.

Answers: 1. basketball hoop 2. plant in bed 3. in-line skates 4. lamp 5. Elisha's handstand

Three in a Row

- -

Materials: • copies of this page, one for each child and one more • scissors • crayons • glue • colored marshmallows • poster board

Preparation: Cut out a set of cards for each child. Color and cut out one set of cards for yourself.

Directions: 1. Children each color their set of cards, and then glue them on a sheet of the poster board in any pattern. 2. As children color, place your cards face-down on a table. 3. One at a time, show each card. As you do, assist the children in covering the correct one on their game boards with a marshmallow.

What to Say: What does a (baby) have to do with our Bible story? Repeat, asking similar questions for each card as it is revealed. **The first person to get three in a row get to lead us in saying the memory verse!**

Suggested Usage: Have extra marshmallows on hand because many will be eaten during the game!

Loving Gift

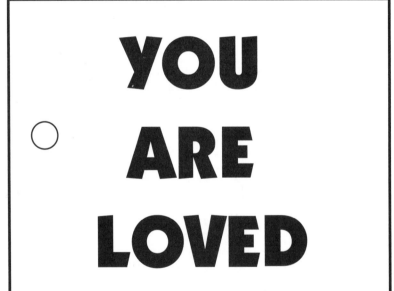

Materials: • copies of this page, one for each child • scissors • green curling ribbon • hole punch
• crayons • pencils, unsharpened • transparent tape • yellow pom-poms • glue

Preparation: Cut out a flower and a tag for each child. Cut a 20-inch piece of ribbon and curl the ends for each child. Punch holes in each tag as indicated.

Directions: 1. Give each child a flower to color. 2. Show how to curve the petals by rolling them on a pencil. 3. Children then tape the flower to the pencil so that the pencil forms a stem. 4. Children glue a pom-pom to the center of the flower. 5. Assist children to thread ribbon through tag and tie tag to each flower stem (pencil). 6. Use a pair of scissors to curl the ends of the ribbons.

What to Say: When we give gifts to people we make them feel loved. The Shunemite couple made Elisha feel loved when they gave him the special room. Elisha made them feel loved when he gave them the baby. We can make someone feel loved by giving them this gift.

Loving Partners

Materials: • copies of this page, one for every eight children • scissors

Preparation: Cut out the hearts and split by cutting on the lines.

Directions: 1. As each child arrives, hand them half a heart. 2. Children find the child who has the other half of their heart to be their partners for the class.

Chapter 22
Naaman

 ## Memory Verse

Be happy with what you have. Hebrews 13:5

Story to Share

Naaman, the great leader of Syria's army, had a terrible disease. It was called leprosy. His wife was very sad.

"Why are you crying?" asked her maid.

"Oh, it is just terrible. Naaman has the dreaded disease. He has leprosy," she answered before covering her face with her hands and sobbing.

"Don't cry," said the little maid. "I know a great prophet, Elisha. He could cure your husband."

Naaman left on a journey to Elisha's home. Elisha sent his servant Gehazi to tell Naaman what to do: "Elisha says to go wash in the Jordan River seven times. Then your skin will be pure."

Naaman obeyed Elisha's orders and his skin became like that of a young boy. He was cured. Naaman was so thankful he tried to give Elisha some magnificent presents. "Thank you for helping to cure me of my leprosy," he said as he handed the gifts to Elisha. "I know your God must be the true God. Take these gifts and gold as my thank-you."

"No," said Elisha. "I don't want your gifts. May God bless you as you return to your home."

Gehazi heard Naaman offer Elisha the gifts. He wanted those beautiful presents! I'll just wait until Naaman is out of sight, he thought. Then I will go get the gifts.

That's what he did. As soon as Naaman was out of Elisha's sight, he hurried to him. "My master has changed his mind," he lied. "He would like the gifts and gold."

But God helped Elisha to know about Gehazi's sin. "You will have the curse of leprosy because you are not content with what you have," he told him.

Elisha knew how to be content with what God had given him. He was God's child.

—*based on 2 Kings 5:15–27*

Discussion Questions

1. Was Gehazi satisfied with what he already had?
2. How do you feel about your toys, clothes, and home? Are you satisfied with what you have?

Be Happy

Materials: • copies of this page, one for each child • scissors • crayons • glue • craft sticks

Preparation: Cut out the bee and toy patterns, making one set for each child.

Directions: 1. Children color the bee and toys. 2. Children glue craft sticks to the ends of the bee and toys.

What to Say: Say the memory verse, holding up the bee for "be" and the toys for "happy." **How many of you have a toy box with toys in it? Maybe you keep your toys in your drawers or closet. Is there some toy you are wishing for? God tells us to be happy with the toys we have. It's okay to get a new toy once in a while, but you shouldn't fuss for something new on each trip to a store. Remember, "Be happy."**

Buzzing Happy Bees

finished craft

Materials: • copies of this page, one for each child plus one more • scissors • resealable plastic bag • glue • yellow round balloons

Preparation: Cut out the stripes and eye patterns, and place each set in a resealable plastic bag. Inflate a balloon for each child. Hint: Do not inflate the balloons to their fullest size to help prevent popping. Have extra inflated balloons on hand just in case. Follow directions below to make a sample.

Directions: 1. Show where to glue the eyes and stripes on the balloons (see illustration). 2. Help each child trace their hands onto a sheet of black construction paper and cut out to make wings. 3. Children glue wings to the back of their bee.

What to Say: As children work, lead them to repeat with you, **Buzz, buzz, be happy. Buzz, buzz, be happy.**

Full Hearts

Materials: • copy of this page enlarged by 200 percent • copies of this page, one for every two children • brown paper grocery bags • scissors • yarn • crayons • glue • staplers • fiberfill stuffing • hole punch

Preparation: Cut out and trace the heart onto brown paper grocery bags, tracing two hearts for each child. Cut out hearts and Jesus figures. Cut yarn into 8-inch lengths.

Directions: 1. Give each child two brown-paper hearts, a Jesus figure, and a length of yarn 2. Children color and then glue a Jesus figure to the middle of a heart. 3. Help children staple the edges of their hearts together, leaving a 3-inch opening. 4. Assist children in stuffing fiberfill in the hole and then stapling the hole closed. 5. Punch a hole on the top of each heart. Thread yarn through the hole and tie into a loop for hanging.

What to Say: Our hearts remind us that when we join God's family, our hearts become so full that we don't have room for the "I wants."

Naaman's Spots

Materials: • copy of Naaman on this page enlarged by 200 percent • copies of this page to make one leprosy spot for each child • scissors • masking tape • sticky tack • crayons • blindfold

Preparation: Cut out Naaman. Post Naaman on a wall. Cut out one leprosy spot per child. Make masking-tape loops.

Directions: 1. Children color Naaman. 2. Assist children in printing their initials on their leprosy spot. Place a masking-tape loop on the back of each spot. 3. Children take turns being blindfolded to try and put their spot on Naaman.

Chapter 23
Jericho

Memory Verse

We will obey him. Joshua 24:24

Story to Share

"God, show me what to do," prayed
Joshua. "I am nearing Jericho.
How can we conquer the city with those high, high walls?"

God told Joshua what to do. But what a strange command God gave him!
Would it really work? Joshua didn't hesitate, he went right to the captains
of his army. "God has told me how to conquer Jericho," he said.

When the captains heard what God said, they agreed: "It is
very strange, but we will do what God has commanded."

The next day all of the soldiers of Joshua's army lined up. Joshua
led the army in a line around the city of Jericho as God commanded.
They marched all around the city and they did not say a word. There
were hundreds and hundreds of soldiers and they were all quiet.

For six days the soldiers marched around the city and for six days they
were quiet. On the seventh day, Joshua's army marched around the city
seven times. Seven times around and not one sound was heard! But then,
the trumpets blew and the soldiers yelled as loud as they could.

As all the noise hit the air, the walls of Jericho came tumbling
down. The soldiers rushed into the city and destroyed it.

The walls fell down because Joshua obeyed God. He was God's child.

—based on Joshua 5:13—6:26

Discussion Questions

1. Is it always easy to obey?
2. Should we always obey?
3. Who in our Bible story obeyed God?

Obedient Joshua

Around and around the army went   **March in place.**

Shh, shh, don't say a word.   **Finger to lips.**

One, two, three, four, five, six days.   **Count on fingers.**

Around and around not a sound was heard.   **March in place.**

On day seven the army marched around.   **March in place.**

Shh, Shh, don't say a word.   **Finger to lips.**

Seven times, shh, shh, don't say a word.   **Hold up seven fingers.**

Around and around not a sound was heard.   **March in place.**

Then the trumpets sounded: Toot, toot, toot.   **Play pretend trumpet.**

The army men shouted: Yeah, yeah, yeah.   **Hands to mouth.**

The walls fell down: Crash, crash, crash.   **Clap hands.**

What a happy, happy day.   **Big smiles.**

Suggested Usage: Direct the class to form a circle. Demonstrate the rhyme first, repeating it several times.

Edible Walls

We will obey him.

Joshua 24:24

We will
obey him.
Joshua 24:24

Materials: • copies of this page, one for each child plus one more • scissors • toothpicks • glue • graham crackers
• canned icing • waxed paper • plastic knives • large marshmallows

Preparation: Cut out flags. Follow directions below to make a sample snack for children to refer to as they work.

Directions: 1. Help children form walls and a roof with the graham crackers squares and icing. 2. Show the
children how to fold a flag in half and glue it around a toothpick. 3. Children stick the flag in a marshmallow, spread
a small amount of icing on the bottom of the marshmallow, and stick it to center of the "roof."

God's Soldiers

We will obey him.

Joshua 24:24

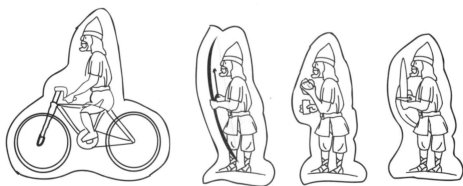

Materials: • copies of this page, one for each child • scissors • crayons • glue

Preparation: Cut out the walled Jericho pictures and figures.

Directions: Children color the pictures. Children choose the soldiers who are being obedient and glue them in place on the picture.

What to Say: When you obey your parents, you do exactly what they tell you to do. When Joshua's soldiers obeyed God, they did exactly what God told Joshua they should do. How can we obey God better?

Obedience Puzzle

Preparation: Cut puzzles out, making one for each child. Place each puzzle in a resealable plastic sandwich bag.

Directions: 1. Children put their puzzle together and color it. 2. Children place puzzle pieces back in bag to take home and use as they retell the story to their family.

Suggested Usage: This is a good project for free time at the beginning or end of your class session. Place a couple puzzles on a table for those who arrive early or those whose parents are late picking them up.

Chapter 24

Ruth

 Memory Verse

Give thanks to [God]. Psalm 100:4

Story to Share

Ruth and Naomi were moving. They were moving from Moab to Bethlehem. "Ruth, my dear daughter-in-law, you do not need to move with me," said Naomi. "You have lived in Moab all your life."

"Naomi," said Ruth, "I am moving with you. When I married your son I learned to love the same God you serve. Now my husband is dead, but I love you and I want to move with you back to Bethlehem."

The two women traveled on, finally reaching the town that sat up on a hill. What excitement there was in the little town when the people saw Naomi.

"Naomi! We're so glad to see you," said one.

"Naomi, it's good to see you back home where you belong," another told her.

Naomi was so glad to be back in Bethlehem. But there was the responsibility of finding food for the two of them. "Naomi, don't you worry about our food," Ruth told her. "It's the time of barley harvest. You have told me God's people always leave some grain standing for the poor. I'll go to the fields tomorrow and gather the barley that is left."

Boaz owned the fields where Ruth went to pick the barley. He had heard how kind she had been to travel all the distance with Naomi and take care of her.

"Come and eat our food for lunch," said Boaz. "You will be safe here and you may gather all the barley you need."

Ruth's heart was happy because of Boaz's kindness. "Thank you, thank you," she told him.

That night, when Ruth told Naomi what Boaz had said, Naomi said, "Ruth, let us thank God for taking care of us."

Together the two women thanked God for being so good to them. "Thank you, God, thank you," Ruth said again.

—based on Ruth 2:8–17

Discussion Questions

1. What has God done for you that you are thankful for?
2. How can we show our thanks?

Gathering Wheat Puzzle

Give thanks to [God]. Psalm 100:4

Materials: • card-stock copies of this page, two for each child • scissors • crayons • resealable plastic sandwich bags
Preparation: Cut out two puzzles for each child. For half the puzzles, cut out the individual pieces. Keep the other puzzles intake. Place the individual puzzle pieces in a pile in the center of the table where children will be working.
Directions: 1. Hand each child an intake puzzle to color. 2. Children find puzzle pieces from the pile to place on top of

Cups of Thanks

I thank you for my food,
And for the sunshine bright.
I thank you for your love,
You show both day and night.

Materials: • card-stock copies of this page, one for each child • scissors • crayons • cooking magazines • glue

Directions: 1. Assist children as they cut out prayer card and fold on the dotted line.

2. Children tear or cut out pictures of food from magazines and glue to prayer cards.

What to Say: Just like God provided food for Ruth and Naomi, he provides food for you.

Place this card on your dinner table to remember to thank God for what He has given you.

Thankful Worksheet

Give thanks to [God]. Psalm 100:4

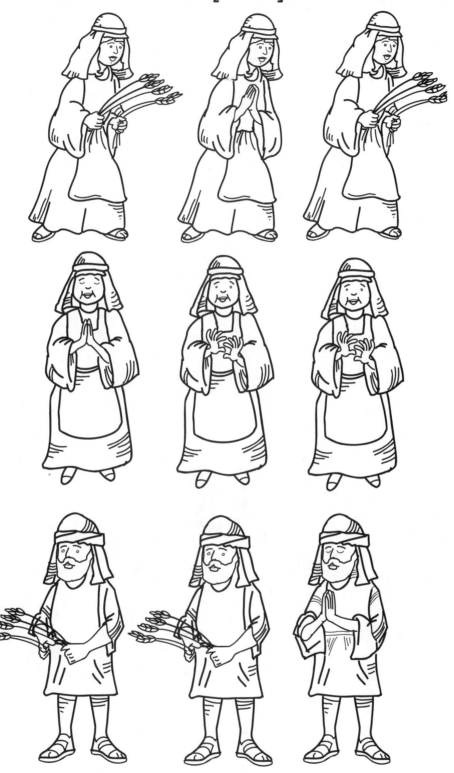

Materials: • copies of this page, one for each child   • crayons

Directions: 1. In each row, children circle the picture that is different. 2. Children color the page.

What to Say: It looks like Ruth, Naomi, and Boaz all knew our memory verse, Psalm 100:4. Let's say the words together, "Give thanks to [God]."

I'm Thankful For . . .

Give thanks to [God]. Psalm 100:4

Materials: • copies of this page, one for each child • crayons

Directions: 1. Children draw what they are thankful for in the prayer cloud. 2. Children color the page.

What to Say: Discuss with children the things they are thankful for. **Do you have a pet you are thankful for? A bed you slept in last night? Do you like the warm sunshine or the twinkling stars?**

Chapter 25
Samuel

**Memory Verse**

I have promised to obey your words. Psalm 119:57

Story to Share

Eli the high priest had two sons, Hophni and Phinehas, who were greedy and selfish. They did not show respect for God's house or for their father, Eli.

Unlike Hophni and Phineas, Samuel was a good helper to Eli. God had blessed Samuel's mother, Hannah, so she raised Samuel to love God. When Samuel was old enough, she took him to Eli. There were many chores Samuel could do for Eli, such as sweeping the floor and filling the lamps with oil.

Eli loved Samuel. He often would tell Samuel stories about God.

One night Samuel woke up to hear, "Samuel, Samuel." Samuel quickly got up and ran to Eli.

"I did not call you, Samuel," Eli told him. "Go back to sleep."

Then it happened a second time: "Samuel, Samuel," he heard. But Eli again said it wasn't him.

When Samuel went to Eli the third time, the priest knew who was calling Samuel. "If you hear your name again," said Eli, "say, 'Speak, Lord, for your servant is listening.'"

When Samuel heard his name again, he answered, "Speak, Lord, for your servant is listening."

God then told Samuel to tell Eli that his sons were evil: "They have cursed me and disobeyed my commands. They will be punished."

The next morning Samuel told Eli what God had said to him. "The Lord is right," Eli said. "My sons have sinned and I did not stop them. If only they would have obeyed God rather than doing what they wanted."

Hophni and Phinehas were killed in a battle with the Philistines. They were punished for their disobedience.

—*based on Samuel 1—3*

Discussion Questions

1. What did Hophni and Phinehas tell Eli when Eli asked them to obey God?

2. What should you do when your parents ask you to obey?

Counting 1, 2, 3

☐	How many times did Samuel go to Eli in the night?
☐	How many sons did Eli have?
☐	How many Samuels lived with Eli?

One, two, three,   *Hold up fingers as you count.*
Tells the story, you see.
Obedient like Samuel,
That's what I'll be!

Materials: • copies of this page, one for each child • scissors • pencils • crayons • glue
Preparation: Cut out a set of questions and a set of numbers for each child.
Directions: 1. Read the words on the left to the children. 2. Help children find the correct number and glue it to the dashed-line box.
What to Say: Recite the poem on the page. Encourage children to count with you, "1, 2, 3."

Erase-a-Smile

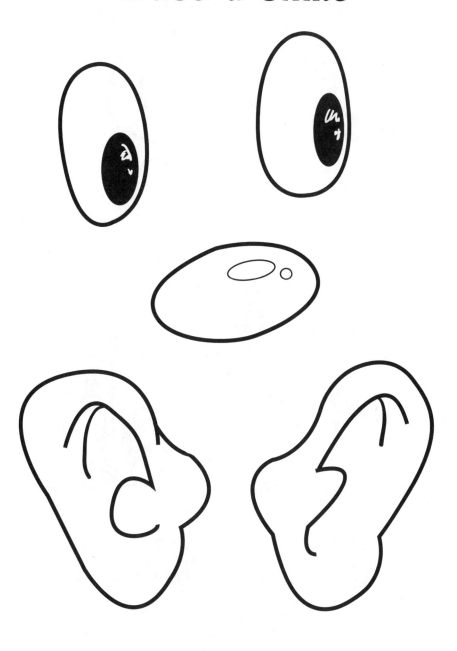

Materials: • copies of this page, one for each child and one extra • scissors • tempera paint in skin tones (pink, peach, brown, tan)
• resealable plastic sandwich bags • duct tape • tempera paint in skin tones (pink, peach, brown, tan) • crayons • glue

Preparation: Cut out each set of facial features. For each child and yourself, partially fill a sandwich bag with paint. Push the air out of each bag, seal, and then secure the seal with duct tape. Follow directions below to create a sample craft.

Directions: 1. Give each child a prefilled bag of paint. 2. Children color and glue the facial features to their paint bags.

What to Say: I'm going to read some sentences about kids. If the child is being obedient, use your fingers to draw smiles on your bag face. If the child is not being obedient, draw a frown. Use the sample you prepared to demonstrate how to make a smile and a frown. **Mommy told Jacob to pick up his blocks. Jacob looked at a book instead.** (Frown.)
Carli's aunt told her not to eat a cookie before dinner. Carli put the spoons on the table instead. (Smile.) **Daddy told Carson to get into bed. Carson jumped in and pulled the covers over his head.** (Smile.) **The Bible says, "Don't tell a lie." Elena told her mother the truth when she broke a glass plate.** (Smile.) **Mr. Shawn said, "Don't touch the paint." Dustin got too close and got paint on his fingers.** (Frown.)

Obedience Lesson

Materials: • copy of this page, enlarged to 300 percent, one for every six children • scissors • crayons
Preparation: Cut out the pictures.
Directions: Children color pictures.
What to Say: Our verse says, "I have promised to obey your words." Who should we obey? Children respond. Hold up each picture and discuss obeying that person. Hold up the question mark. **Do you have trouble being obedient?** Pray, asking God to help the children to be obedient.

Samuel's Robe Mobile

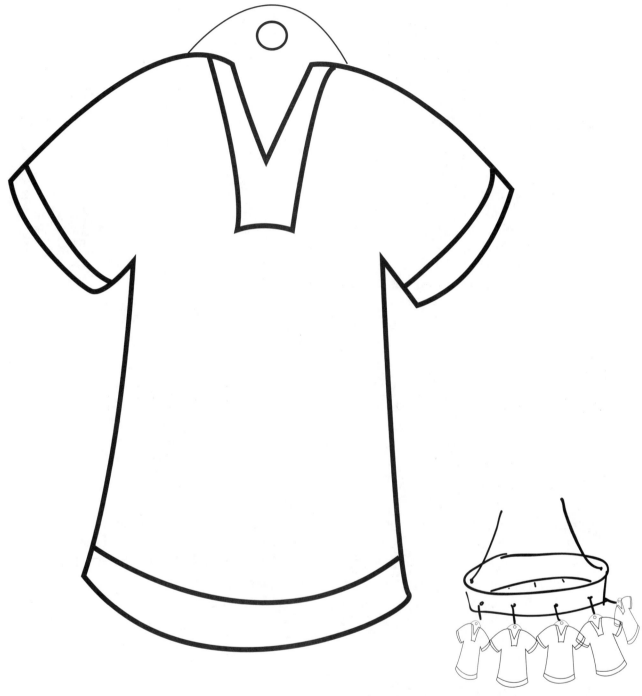

finished craft

Materials: • copies of this page, one for each child • scissors • poster board • hole punch • crayons • yarn

Preparation: Duplicate and cut out a robe for each child. Create a mobile bar from two strips of poster board. Punch holes on the mobile bar, as shown in the sketch. Cut yarn into 6- to 8-inch lengths. Tie an approximately 3-foot length of yarn to the top of the bar for hanging.

Directions: 1. Give each child a robe and instruct the children to color their robes with their favorite colors. 2. As each child finishes, print child's name on the back of the robe. 3. Punch a hole in the neck of each robe and tie a piece of yarn to the hole. Tie the free end of the yarn to one of the holes in the mobile bar. 4. Hang the finished mobile where the children can enjoy it.

What to Say: When Samuel went to live in the temple, his mommy brought him a new robe every year. We're going to color robes to make a colorful mobile to hang in our room. Our mobile will help us remember to obey God. As you print each child's name on the back of their robe and say, **Just like Samuel, (Justin) can choose to obey God.**

Chapter 26
Nehemiah

Memory Verse

Keep your hands busy. Ecclesiastes 11:6

Story to Share

Nehemiah had an important job. He served wine to the Persian king, Artaxerxes. But Nehemiah was also a Jew and Jerusalem was his heart's home. One day when some men came from Judea he asked them, "How is Jerusalem?"

Nehemiah was sad when he heard their answer. "The people are poor, they are disrespected, and the city wall is broken down," the men told Nehemiah.

So Nehemiah asked King Artaxerxes if he could go rebuild the city of Jerusalem. He found it just as the men had told him. Not only was the wall broken, the gates had been burned. It would take many men to rebuild the city but Nehemiah knew that many hands could get the work done. Each family was asked to build part of the wall. "Yes," they agreed. "We will help."

The enemies of Jerusalem were angry when they saw the wall being rebuilt. They liked to be able to get into the city and steal the crops from the Israelite people. These enemies threatened Nehemiah and his men. Nehemiah gathered the people of Jerusalem all together. "Don't be afraid," he said. "God is with us and will protect us."

Nehemiah gave some of the workmen spears and shields. They protected the men who were working on the wall. All those hands kept busy for fifty-two days. Then the work was done, the gates could be closed, and guards were posted there. Because of all the hard work, the people of Israel could be safe in their towns and villages.

—based on Nehemiah 1–6

Discussion Questions

1. Do you like to work together with your mommy or a friend?
2. How can you use your hands for Jesus?

What Is Nehemiah Building?

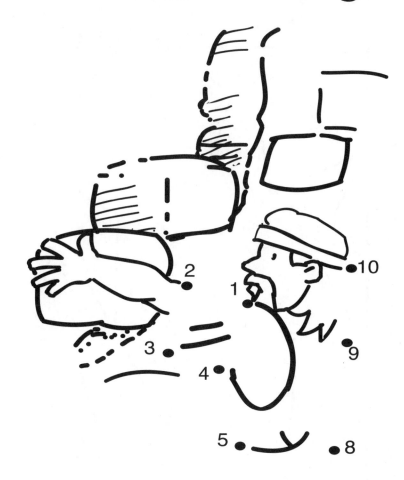

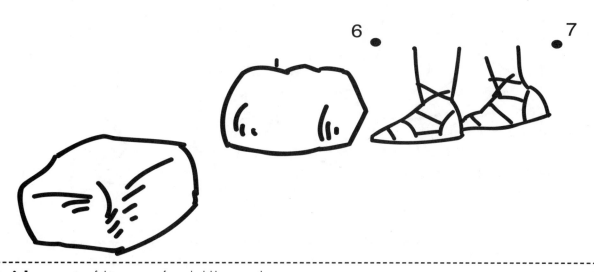

Materials: • copies of this page, one for each child • pencils • crayons

Directions: Children connect the dots from 1–10 and color picture.

What to Say: Encourage children to start at number 1 and say the numbers aloud with you as they draw from dot to dot.

Use Them!

Color the hearts red and the stars blue to see the surprise.

Materials: • copies of this page, one for each child • crayons

Directions: 1. Read coloring instructions to children. 2. Children color page according to instructions.

What to Say: There is a hidden shape in this picture. It is something that Jesus wants you to use. What is it?

Handy Reminder

Keep your
hands busy.

Ecclesiastes 11:6

Keep your
hands busy.
Ecclesiastes 11:6

finished craft

Materials: • copies of this page, one for each child plus one more • scissors • yarn • hole punch
• clear plastic lids, one for each child • bright crayons • facial tissues • glue
Preparation: Cut out hands. Cut six-inch lengths of yarn, one for each hand. Punch a hole near the top
of each lid. Color one of the hands with a brightly color crayon, pressing down firmly.
Directions: 1. Children color the hand pattern with a brightly color crayon, pressing down firmly. 2. Demonstrate how to rub the colored hand
with tissues until it is smooth and shiny. 3. Children glue the hand to a lid. 4. Make a hanger by tying a length of yarn to each lid.

Marshmallow Walls

Materials: • large marshmallows • frosting • plastic knives and spoons
Directions: 1. Children wash and dry hands. 2. Children work together to build a rectangle with marshmallow walls at least three marshmallows high. 3. If the walls keep falling down, have children use some frosting to stick them together.
What to Say: It was a lot of hard work for God's people to build all the walls of Jerusalem up again. They used really large rocks to make it safe and secure. When we work together we can do many things for God. How can you use your hands for Jesus?

Chapter 27

Jesus' Birth

Memory Verse

I have given you an example. John 13:15

Story to Share

To Mary, the trip from Nazareth to Bethlehem seemed
like it would never end. But the trip was necessary.
The king's law required the people to go back to the
land where they were born so they could be taxed.

Clip, clop, clip, clop. The donkey's feet
moved in rhythm and bounced Mary as she rode him. Joseph walked by her.
He smiled when she glanced at him. "Almost there," he said cheerfully.

But when Joseph and Mary finally reached the town, they found there
were no hotel rooms to rent. Finally an innkeeper offered his stable to the
young couple. Joseph must have spread some clean hay on the floor for his
wife, and then covered it with his coat. Mary was thankful for the soft bed.

Suddenly, it was time for the baby to be born. Joseph made another bed, but this one
was in the manger, where the animals ate. He again placed clean hay in the manger and
covered it with a cloth. When Jesus was born, Mary gently placed the baby in the bed.

Mary and Joseph knew this baby was special. They knew God
had sent his Son into the world to save people from sin.

Jesus grew like other babies. He turned over, he crawled, he walked,
and then he ran! Jesus ate the good foods his mother prepared for him.
As he grew older, he played with his friends and did his chores.

Jesus' earthly father, Joseph, was a carpenter. Joseph taught Jesus to
be a carpenter, too. Jesus listened to his earthly father and obeyed him.

Just like you are growing, Jesus grew healthy, strong,
obedient, and wise. Jesus is a good example for us.

—based on Luke 2:1–7

❓❓❓ Discussion Questions

1. **You probably were born in a hospital. Where was Jesus born?** (Stable.)
2. **How can you grow strong like Jesus?** (Eat healthy foods, run and play, be happy and obedient.)

Clothespin Review

Materials: • copies of this page, one for each child • scissors • resealable plastic sandwich bags • crayons • glue • paper plates • clothespins

Preparation: Cut out a game board and hearts. Please each set in a separate plastic bag, making one set for each child.

Directions: 1. Children color their game boards. 2. Children color one heart for each color: blue, green, red, yellow, purple. 3. Assist children in gluing the game board to a paper plate and hearts to separate clothespins.

What to Say: Retell the story on page 137. As each character or object is introduced, tell the children to clip the colored hearts to the game board: **Clip the yellow heart to Mary, Jesus' mother. Clip the blue heart to Joseph, Jesus' earthly father. Clip the red heart to the stable where Jesus was born. Clip the purple heart to the animals from the stable. Clip the green heart to God's Son, Jesus.**

Stable Sequence Cards

I have given you an example. John 13:15

Materials: • copies of this page and page 140, one for each child • crayons • resealable plastic sandwich bags

Preparation: Cut out a sequence card set for each child. Place each set in a sandwich bag.

Directions: 1. Children color their cards. 2. When you call out a sequence for the cards, children place their cards in that order. Look at each child's cards.

What to Say: Begin by saying the sequence slowly, allowing time for children to place cards after each one is called. Gradually speed up. Repeat each sequence, and if needed, assist by pointing to make sure all children have put their cards in order. Once all the children are correct, lead children to repeat after you, **Jesus is born!**

Continued on next page . . .

Continued from previous page.

Enrichment Idea: After a few rounds, change the play by calling out a sentence that describes one of the cards. Children hold up the appropriate card. 1. An animal that moos; 2. An animal one that is fluffy like cotton; 3. A tiny baby boy. 4. The animal that carried Mary to Bethlehem; 5. The place where Jesus was born; 6. God's Son; 7. An animal that gives milk; 8. Jesus' mother; 9. A home for animals; 10. Jesus' parents (Tricky! This one is two cards); 11. An animal that has feet which say "Clip clop;" 12. An animal that says, "Baaa."

Just Like Me

I have given you an example.

John 13:15

Materials: • copies of this page, one for each child   • crayons
Directions: 1. Children draw a line from the pictures of Jesus on the left to a corresponding picture
on the right of a modern child doing the same action. 2. Children color the pictures.
What to Say: What kinds of things do you do for play time that Jesus might have done? (Tell jokes, hang out with
friends, play games, etc.) **How was Jesus a good example for us? God wants us to try to be like Jesus.**

Chapter 28
Jesus as a Boy in the Temple

 **Memory Verse**

Children, obey your parents. Colossians 3:20

 Story to Share

When Jesus was twelve years old, he was preparing to become a Jewish adult. He went with Mary and Joseph to Jerusalem for the Festival of the Passover.

Before they knew it, it was time to return home to Nazareth. Many people were traveling together. Thinking that Jesus was with the other children, Mary and Joseph asked one group of children, "Have you seen Jesus?"

"No, not since we left Jerusalem," the children said.

Mary and Joseph found another group of children. "Is Jesus with you?"

"No, we haven't seen him today."

For three days Mary and Joseph hunted for their son. Finally, they went to the temple, and quickly looked over the crowd. "Look, Mary, I see him."

"Where, where is he?" asked Mary, her eyes following Joseph's pointing finger. And there he was! He was sitting in the middle of a group of teachers, talking to them, listening to what they had to say, asking them questions.

"Jesus," said Mary touching him on the shoulder. "Where have you been?"

"He's been here," said one of the men. "We've been amazed with the wisdom and understanding of your twelve-year-old."

"Yes, Mother and Father. I have been right here," Jesus agreed. "You didn't need to search for me. You should have known I would be in my Father God's house."

Joseph shook his head. "You are right, Jesus. We should have known. But it is time to come home with us to Nazareth."

Jesus quickly stood to his feet. "Yes, Father. I am ready."

Mary, Joseph, and Jesus returned home. Jesus obeyed his parents at home as he did in the temple.

—based on Luke 2:42–51

Discussion Questions

1. Did Jesus obey his parents quickly?

2. Do you say "wait a minute" when your mother or father calls?

The Obedient Way

Use a red crayon to help Mary and Joseph find Jesus. Use a blue crayon to help Jesus obey Mary and Joseph so they can find their way back home.

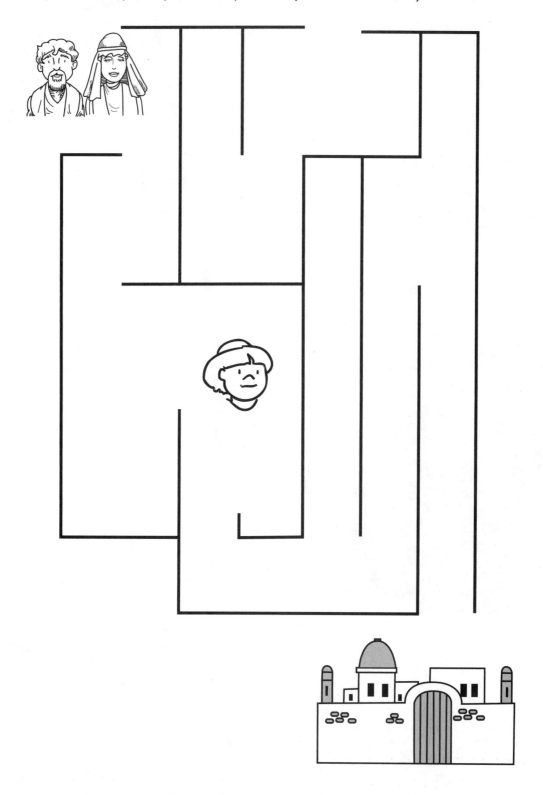

Materials: • copies of this page, one for each child • crayons, red and blue
Directions: 1. Read instructions aloud and assist children to complete both directions in the maze. 2. Children color the page.

Obedience Is Blooming

Materials: • copies of this page, one for each child • scissors • resealable plastic sandwich bags
• glue • large sheet of poster board • crayons • yellow pom-poms

Preparation: Cut out one flower center, and all the suns and flower petals. Place three suns and one flower petal in each plastic bag to make one set for each child. Glue the flower center to the middle of the poster-board sheet. Print "Obedience Is Blooming" at the top of the poster board.

Directions: 1. Assist children to write their names in the center of their flower petal and then color the petal. 2. Children glue their petals to the poster board, around the flower center, to make a flower. 3. Children color their suns yellow and glue around the edge of the poster board. 4. Children help you glue the pom-poms to fill in the flower center.

I Will Obey

Materials: • copies of this page, one for each child • crayons

Directions: 1. Children color the pictures. 2. Children follow along as you give them the verbal instructions below.

What to Say: **Let's help Mike and Molly obey and do the chores I say. Molly, please put the books back on the book shelf.** Lead children to say, "I will obey" and draw a line from the books to Molly. Children continue saying "I will obey" and drawing lines as you indicate in your instructions. **Mike, please set the table. Molly, please take the dog for a walk. Mike, please pick up your toys. Mike, please wash your hands.**

Flower Garden

Children, obey your parents. Colossians 3:20

Materials: • card-stock copies of this page, one for each child • crayons • craft
sticks • glue • variety of colorful paper cupcake liners • glitter glue
Preparation: Cut the craft sticks in half, making five halves for each child.
Directions: 1. Children color the sun yellow and the leaves green on their paper. 2. Each child colors three craft-
stick halves green and then glue them to the paper to make stalks. 3. Each child glues a cupcake liner to the top of
each craft stick to make a flower. 4. Children use glitter glue to decorate the center of their flowers.

Patchwork Comfort Card

Jesus' loving concern will warm your heart!

[God] will also show loving concern.
Lamentations 3:32

_____

(Inside of card)

Materials: • card-stock copies of this page, one for each child plus one • scissors • 1-inch fabric squares • glue

Preparation: Cut out the cards. Follow the instructions below to make a sample card.

Directions: 1. Children glue fabric squares on the front of the card to resemble a quilt. 2. Assist the children as needed to print their names on the lines inside their cards. 3. Arrange to take the children to a class for older church members, to a nursing home, Or gather the cards and deliver them yourself. Be sure to take pictures of the elderly with the cards to show the children.

What to Say: When you are sick or sad you probably like to cuddle up in a warm blanket. Jesus' comfort can be like putting a quilt on your heart. It makes you feel warm and loved!

Giving Comfort

- -

Materials: • copies of this page, one for each child • crayons

Directions: 1. One at a time, discuss the pictures on the worksheet. Help children identify the pictures in which someone is showing compassion. 2. Children color the pictures that show compassion and draw a red X through the pictures that do not show compassion. 3. As needed, help children print their names in the hearts.

What to Say: Sometimes Jesus uses us to give comfort. Can you see someone in the pictures giving comfort? If you want Jesus to use you to show his compassion, take your red crayon and color the heart in the middle of the page. Now print your name in the heart.

Story People

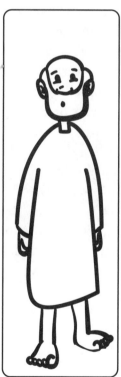 

Materials: • copies of this page, one for each child plus one more • scissors • resealable plastic sandwich bag
• crayons • gauze, cut in ½-inch strips • spring-type clothespins • glue

Preparation: Cut out a set of story figures for each child. Place the figures in separate plastic bags. Follow directions below to make a sample set of figures.

Directions: 1. Children color the story pictures. 2. Help the children glue the story pictures on the clothespins, so that the figures will appear to be standing when the clothespin stands on its ends. 3. Give each child a piece of gauze to wrap around Lazarus.

What to Say: Retell the story using the figures to act it out. Encourage children to act out the story with their figures.

Chapter 30
Feeding the 5,000

Memory Verse

God did miracles . . . through Jesus. Acts 2:22

Story to Share

Jesus was tired. He had been preaching to crowds and healing the sick for many, many days.

"Let's get away and rest," Jesus told the disciples. So they got on their boat and sailed across the Galilee Sea.

But Jesus didn't get much time to rest. The people saw where he was heading and thousands followed him because they knew he could heal them.

Jesus saw them. He saw that they needed healing and needed to be taught about God. Jesus spent much of the day talking to the crowd and healing those who needed it.

A small boy in the crowd saw Jesus doing these miracles. He saw a man who had a bad leg now walking around. He saw a blind woman looking with joy at her young son. He saw Jesus touch the ears of a man who couldn't hear—and then the man suddenly began to hear and talk!

This small boy knew Jesus was God's Son. When the disciples began looking for food for the people, he looked at his small lunch of five barley rolls and two small fish. It wasn't much, but he wanted to give it to Jesus—the miracle man!

Jesus took the boy's small lunch and thanked God for it. Then he told the disciples to pass the food around to all the people. The boy watched as the food turned into enough for everyone to eat—and there were twelve baskets left over. All from his tiny lunch!

The young boy gave what he had to help Jesus. So can we.

—based on Mark 6:30–44

Discussion Questions

1. **Why did the little boy know Jesus could use his small lunch?** (He saw Jesus perform many other miracles.)
2. **Jesus still performs miracles today. What is a miracle Jesus has done during your life?** Be prepared to share an age-appropriate example from your own life.

Bible Story Cards

The Miracle of a Small Boy's Lunch

1

2

3

4

5

Materials: • copies of this page, one for each child   • scissors   • resealable plastic sandwich bag, one per child   • felt   • crayons

Preparation: Cut out a set of story pictures for each child. Place each set in a separate plastic bag.

Directions: 1. Children color the pictures. 2. As you retell the story, children arrange the pictures of Jesus' miracle in the correct order. 3. Children return pictures to plastic bag to take home so they can retell the story to their family members and friends.

Count the Fish

Materials: • copies of this page, one for each child • crayons
Directions: Children find the people and baskets with matching numbers, and color both the same color.
What to Say: How many fish did the boy bring to Jesus? How do you think the boy felt about sharing his food? It must have seemed like it wasn't enough to feed so many people, but the boy shared anyway. How did Jesus show God's power?

Chapter 31
The Good Samaritan

Memory Verse

"Love the Lord" . . . and *"love your neighbor."* Luke 10:27

Story to Share

A man asked Jesus, "What do I need to do to live with you in Heaven?" Jesus said, "What is written in God's Word? You should know."

The man knew. He answered. "It says, 'Love the Lord your God with all your heart . . . and love your neighbor.'"

Jesus said, "That is right. That's what God wants you to do."

The man asked another question. "Who is my neighbor?" So Jesus told a story. He said a man was traveling. Some robbers beat him up and stole his money. He was very badly hurt and they left him lying on the side of the road. As he lay there hurt, a man from his own country saw him and crossed the street to go around him and not help. Another man from his country did the same thing. He saw he was hurt and crossed the street to not pass right by him. These two men knew about God and did not stop and show love to help him.

Then a Samaritan came along. He was from another country. The people from his country didn't like the people from the country the hurt man was from. It was unusual for people from these two places to help each other. But, the Samaritan saw how hurt he was and couldn't leave the injured man there to die. He put bandages on the man and then took him on a donkey to an inn. He took good care of the injured man. Even after the kind Samaritan man had to leave, he left money for the innkeeper to continue to take care of the hurt man until he was well.

Jesus asked, "Which of these three men do you think was a neighbor to the injured man?"

Of course, the answer was, "The Samaritan, who helped the hurt man." Jesus told them to go and show the same love and kindness to others. Jesus wants us to show love and kindness to the people in our lives, too.

—based on Luke 10:25–37

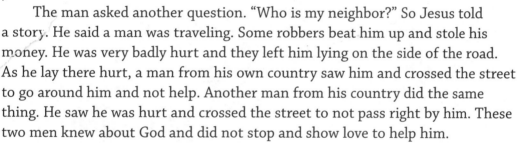

Discussion Questions

1. What does God's Word say for us to do?
2. Why was the Samaritan a good neighbor?

Stand-Up Story Triangle

Materials: • copies of this page, one for each child plus one more • scissors • crayons • transparent tape

Preparation: Cut out story patterns. Follow directions below to make a sample.

Directions: 1. Children color the pictures. 2. Help children fold the stand-up story triangle on the dashed lines and tape at the seam.

What to Say: Retell the story, turning the triangle to the various scenes as you tell the story.

We can love our neighbors and find ways to be kind to them.

Suggested Usage: Invite another class to enjoy a snack. Tell the Bible story to your visitors, as children demonstrate how to use the stand-up story triangle.

Love Your Neighbor

To the tune of "Are You Sleeping?"

"Love your neighbor,"
"Love your neighbor,"
Jesus said.
Jesus said.
I can love my neighbor.
I can love my neighbor.
You can, too.
You can, too.

I
point to self

Love
cross hands over heart

You
point to another person

Materials: • copies of this page, one for each child.

Directions: 1. Teach children the "Love Your Neighbor" song and motions, singing to the tune of "Are You Sleeping?" 2. Children color the picture.

I Love You Hearts

I Love You!

"Love the Lord" . . . and
"love your neighbor."
Luke 10:27

Materials: • copies of this page, one for each child • scissors • crayons • large (larger than 6 inches wide) paper lace doilies, any color • glue
Preparation: Cut out a heart for each child.
Directions: 1. Children color their hearts. 2. Help children glue the heart to a paper doily.
Optional: For older children, spread some glue inside the letters and then sprinkle glitter or colored sand on the glue.
What to Say: Give this heart to someone to tell them you love them.

Chapter 32
Peter Preaches

Memory Verse

Blessed are those who suffer for doing what is right. Matthew 5:10

Story to Share

After Jesus went back to Heaven, more people chose to follow Jesus. God's church was growing bigger!

Each day, Peter and some of Jesus' other friends met at the temple gates. They would tell others about Jesus. This made the religious leaders jealous. They hadn't liked Jesus and now they didn't like his friends.

"We need to stop these men from talking about Jesus. No one is listening to us," complained one man.

"Guards," yelled another religious leader, "arrest these friends of Jesus and throw them in prison."

God was with Jesus' friends. God sent an angel to guide them out of prison.

"Come," the angel said. "Don't be afraid to go back to the temple and tell others about Jesus."

Now the leaders were really angry. "Guards, go and get those men NOW!"

When Peter and the other friends of Jesus were brought to the leaders, one of the leaders asked, "Didn't we tell you not to teach about Jesus?"

"Yes," answered Peter. "But we must obey God rather than you. You need to have your sins forgiven by Jesus."

This made the leaders even madder. They started talking about killing Jesus' friends. "Wait," one of the leaders spoke up. "These men are missionaries of Jesus—people who tell others about God. We must be careful to respect them or we will be disrespectful to Jesus."

The leaders were still angry, but knew this man spoke the truth. "Punish them then," they ordered.

When the disciples were released, they were happy in spite of having been hurt. "We suffered for doing what is right and following Jesus," said Peter. "And we will continue to tell others about him."

—*based on Luke 1; Acts 5:17–42*

Discussion Questions

1. **Do you know a missionary who tells others about Jesus?** (Mention missionaries known by your group.)
2. **Who can be a missionary?**

Edible Puzzle

Blessed are
those who
suffer for
doing what
is right.
Matthew 5:10

Materials: • card-stock copies of this page, one for each child • scissors • crayons • pretzel sticks
Preparation: Cut out a puzzle for each child.
Directions: 1. Children color puzzle pieces. 2. Children turn puzzle pieces upside down on the table. 3. On your mark, children race to see who can put the puzzle together the fastest. 4. Children place the pretzel sticks on their completed puzzles to look like bars.
What to Say: Briefly retell the story as children eat the pretzel sticks.

Prayer Chart

_____'s Missionary Prayer Chart

Sunday   Monday   Tuesday   Wednesday   Thursday   Friday   Saturday

Blessed are those who suffer for doing what is right. Matthew 5:10

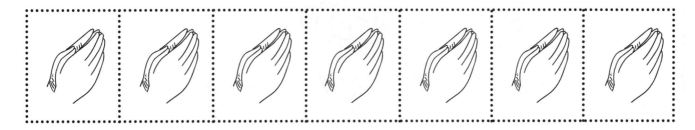

Materials: • copies of this page, one for each child • scissors • envelopes • resealable plastic sandwich bags • crayons • glue

Preparation: Cut out the chart and praying hands. Place a chart, seven praying hands, and an envelope in separate plastic bags to create a set for each child.

Directions: 1. Children color the chart and hands. 2. Help children write their name on the line. 3. Children glue an envelope to the back of the chart and place the praying hands in the envelope. 4. Instruction children to glue on a pair of praying hands each day that they pray for the missionary.

What to Say: This week you can pray for [missionary's name]. Missionaries sometimes suffer for doing what is right by telling others about Jesus. But our verse says that if we suffer for doing what is right, we will be blessed! You can be a missionary by telling a friend about Jesus.

Story Ribbon Bookmark

Materials: • copies of this page, one for each child • construction paper • scissors • crayons • glue
Preparation: Cut the construction paper into 5x11-inch strips, one per child. Use scissors to fringe the short edges of the ribbon.
Directions: 1. Children cut out and color the story pictures. 2. Show how to put the pictures in order and glue them to the strip of fringed construction paper to make a bookmark.

What's Different?

There are ten differences between these two pictures. Circle each difference you find.

Materials: • copies of this page, one for each child • crayons
Directions: Children circle the nine ways the pictures are different from each other and color the picture.
Answers: 1. window 2. smiling soldier 3. length of spear 4. Peter's hat 5. Peter's shoes 6. open door
7. chains on arm 8. angel's sash 9. angel is pointing 10. angel's wings are different shapes

Chapter 33
The Holy Spirit at Pentecost

 Memory Verse

Let us honor him together. Psalm 34:3

Story to Share

One day after Jesus went back to Heaven, the
disciples were meeting together with other believers.
Mary, Jesus' mother, was there with them. There
were about 120 people worshiping God.

Peter, one of Jesus' friends, stood to speak. "Judas
betrayed Jesus," he told the crowd. "Even if he was
alive he would not be worthy to be a disciple." The disciples were the men who followed
Jesus and were his helpers. "We need to decide on someone to take the place of Judas."

The other disciples agreed. The people prayed that they would choose the
right man for this important job. They knew only God could see their hearts.
With his leading, the disciples chose Matthias as the next disciple.

Later, when it was time for Pentecost, a Jewish harvest festival, the disciples
gathered together again. This time while they were worshiping, they heard a sound like
a loud wind. It wasn't the wind blowing from the outside—the sound was in the room!

Suddenly, as they looked at each other they saw what looked like tiny
flames hovering over each of their heads. God had sent the Holy Spirit to them.
This would make it possible for God to speak to them, guide them, and have a
close relationship with him. They were so happy! They were able to understand
everything that was being said by people that even spoke other languages.

People from many different countries had come for the festival. They saw
that God was with the disciples, too. Many people believed in Christ that day—
nearly 3,000! Peter baptized the people who wanted to follow Christ.

—based on Acts 2

Discussion Questions

1. **Where did the disciples go to worship?** (No place in particular, they worshiped anywhere they were, etc.)
2. **Why does God want to talk to you and have a relationship with you?**

Crazy Walks

Materials: • copies of this page, one for each child • crayons
Directions: Children color pages and draw along each dashed line to get the children on the worksheet to church.

Foot Portrait Wall Border

Let	us
honor	him
together.	Psalm 34:3

Materials: • copies of this page, so that there is one square for each child • fluorescent poster board • crayons • scissors • glue
Directions: 1. On fluorescent poster board, each child traces around a foot and cuts out the shape. 2. Children glue a word shape onto their foot and draw a happy face on it. 3. Attach the feet to a wall in verse order.
What to Say: Our feet look happy they came to worship. Do you have a smile on your face, too?

Handy Friendship Wreath

Let us honor him together.

Psalm 34:3

Preparation: Cut out verse circles and hands. Cut a 6-inch circle from poster board, making one for each child plus one extra.
Cut ribbon into 12-inch lengths and tie into a bow, making one for each child. Cut yarn into 8-inch lengths and tie into a loop for
hanging. In separate plastic bags, place one verse circle, six hands, one poster-board circle, and one prepared bow.

Directions: 1. Children glue their verse circles to the poster-board circles. 2. Children glue the hands around the edge, overlapping to fit. 3. Children print their
names on their friends' hands. 4. Give each child a pre-tied bow to glue to the top of the wreath. 5. Tape a yarn hoop to the back of the wreath for hanging.

Lift the Flap Story Picture

6x9-inch construction-paper piece with door

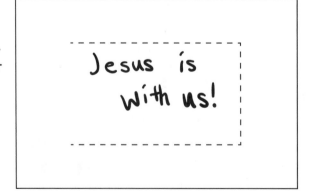

Jesus is with us!

Materials: • copies of this page, one for each child • construction paper • glue • crayons

Preparation: Cut out picture of Jesus, making one for each child. Cut construction paper sheets in half, to make 6x9-inch sheets, two for each child. For half of the 6x9-inch sheets, cut a three-sided door, making one for each child. Print "Jesus is with us!" on the door. (See sketch above.)

Directions: 1. Each child colors a picture. 2. Children glue Jesus pictures to uncut 6x9-inch construction-paper pieces. 3. Children place a cut 6x9-inch construction-paper piece on top and glue construction paper pieces together along the edges. 4. Show the children how to open the doors to see the pictures.

What to Say: Jesus was with his friends when they worshiped together. Jesus is with us, today, while we worship together, too.

Chapter 34

Jesus Clears the Temple Court

Memory Verse

Have respect for my [church]. Leviticus 19:30

Story to Share

Jesus was visiting Jerusalem. The first place he went was the temple. As Jesus stood and looked into the temple courtyard he was shocked at what he saw.

There were people everywhere, and not only people who were coming to God's house to worship him. There were people who were selling animals needed for sacrifices.

"No, no," Jesus heard. "I can't sell you that lamb for so little. You must give me more."

"I don't have more to give you," begged the man who needed the sacrifice. "You are already charging more than I have to give."

Everywhere Jesus turned there was another table with cattle and oxen to be sold. He became angry when he realized that the poor people were going away even poorer because of these greedy people. The poor people had come to the temple to worship God; instead they had their money cheated away from them.

"Get out!" yelled Jesus above the noise of the crowd. "Get out of my house!"

What confusion! What noise! Some of the cattle got loose, birds escaped from their cages and flew around the people's heads, and sheep were "baa"-ing frantically as they tried to escape from the confusion.

Jesus ran to each of the money changer's tables and turned them over. The clanking of coins spilling was heard with the other noise. "This house belongs to my Father," He said. "It is a place to pray but you have made it into a den of robbers."

Jesus didn't stop until all of the livestock sellers were out of the temple. Shaking his head, Jesus said, "What disrespect for the house of God!" Looking around at those who had come to worship, he continued, "Have respect for the temple. This will make me and my Father happy."

—*based on John 2:13–16*

Discussion Questions

1. What is our name for the temple?
2. How should you behave in church?

Respectful Children

Have respect for my [church].
Leviticus 19:30

Song Signs

To the tune of "The More We Get Together"

Oh, I want to be a good friend, a good friend, a good friend,
Oh, I want to be a good friend, good friend in God's house.

I'll zip up my lips	*Pinch index finger and thumb. Run across lips.*
Put my hands on my lap	*Lay hands in lap.*
And my feet will keep together	*Put feet together.*
So my neighbor can hear.	*Cup hands behind ears.*

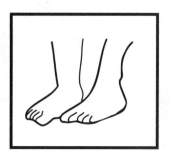

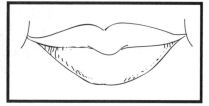

Materials: • card-stock copy of this page, enlarged 300 percent • crayons or markers • glue • craft sticks

Preparation: Cut out and color in the images for the song. Glue a jumbo craft stick to each picture to form a handle, making signs for the song.

Directions: 1. Teach children the song, singing it to the tune of "The More We Get Together." 2. Children take turns holding up the signs.

Suggested Usage: This song can be sung at the beginning of each lesson to remind children to be thoughtful and kind in God's house.

Chapter 35
Jesus Calms the Sea

Memory Verse

I leave my peace with you. John 14:27

Story to Share

"This has been a busy day," Peter said to Jesus. "You have been teaching and healing for hours."

Jesus nodded his head wearily. "Come," Peter urged him. "Let's go for a ride in my boat." Jesus and his disciples entered the boat, thankful for the promise of a quiet ride. Before Peter even picked up his oar to begin to row, Jesus was asleep, curled up in the corner of the boat.

It was getting toward evening, but Peter noticed that the sky seemed darker than usual. The waves began picking up speed and strength. The wind howled eerily.

The disciples looked at each other.

"There's a storm brewing!" Andrew yelled at Peter.

"It's too late to get back to shore in time to miss the storm," Peter yelled back.

Just then, a wave crashed into the boat and water sprayed on their clothes. The waves got fiercer and the wind stronger. The disciples became more frightened as the minutes passed. All through the storm, Jesus slept, exhausted from his day.

Scared, Thomas shook Jesus awake.

"Jesus," he called over the noise of the wind. "Save us, Jesus. We're going to drown."

Jesus rubbed his eyes and looked at the storm.

"Why are you afraid? Where's your faith?" he asked. Then Jesus stretched out his arms, and with his face turned toward the heavens said, "Peace. Be calm."

Instantly, the wind quieted, the waves became soft and gentle, and the sky lightened. Jesus brought peace to a stormy night.

The disciples stared at Jesus. "Even the storms obey his voice," James said.

—based on Matthew 8:23–27

Discussion Questions

1. Who was with the disciples when they were scared? (Jesus.)

2. Are you ever afraid? Who is with you when you are? (Jesus.)

Rocking in the Storm

To the tune of "When the Saints Go Marching."

Oh, when my boat,
Oh, when my boat,
Oh, when my boat rocks in the storm.
I will let Jesus be my captain,
When my boat rocks in the storm.

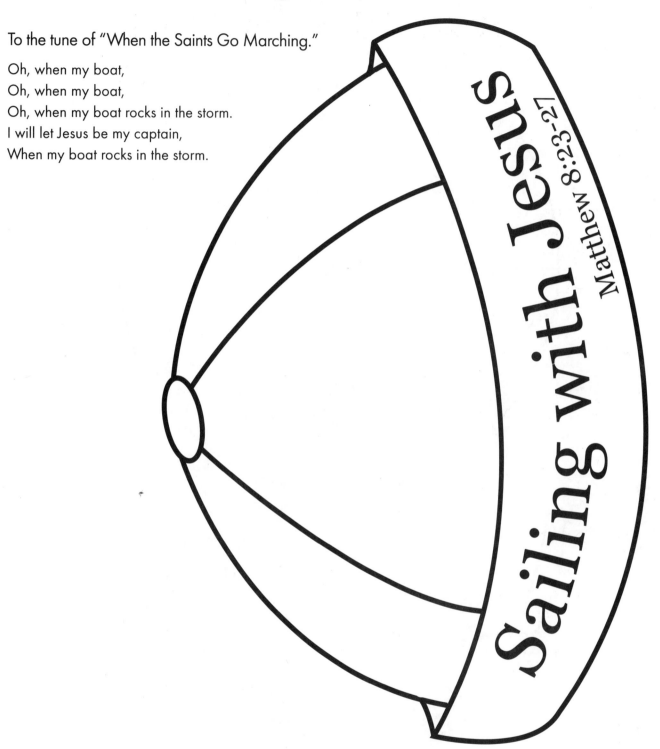

Sailing with Jesus
Matthew 8:23-27

Materials: • card-stock copies of this page, one for each child • scissors • masking tape • star stickers
Preparation: Cut out hats. For each child, make a loop of masking tape.
Directions: 1. Children decorate hats with star stickers. 2. Place a loop of masking tape on the back of each child's hat and stick it to their forehead. Children wear their hats while they sing the "My Rockin' Boat" song to the tune of "When the Saints Go Marching In."

Picture Wheel Boat

I leave my peace with you.

John 14:27

- -

Materials: • copies of this page, one for each child • crayons • brads

Preparation: Cut out a boats and picture wheels.

Directions: 1. Children color the picture wheels and boats. 2. Help children attach the wheel to the boat with a brad.

What to Say: Look at the faces of Jesus' friends. Do they look happy? If they don't look happy, let's turn our wheels. Now they are happy. That's because Jesus gives us peace. Let's say, "Peace, be calm," as we turn our wheels to show Jesus calming the storm.

Jesus Is Captain of My Boat

Materials: • copies of this page, one for each child, and one copy of page 180 • butcher paper • blue paint • paint brush
• crayons • masking tape

Preparation: Cut out a boat for each child. Cut out weather cards on page 180. Paint blue water and waves
on butcher paper and post on a wall. On the poster, print "Jesus Is Captain of My Boat."

Directions: 1. Help children print their name on a boat and color it. 2. Tape the boats to the waves on the board.

What to Say: Which of these weather cards shows what the weather is like today? Tape the appropriate weather card to the poster.

Suggested Usage: Each time you meet, children decide on the weather and attach the appropriate weather card to the poster.

Chapter 36

Jesus Heals

Memory Verse

I look up and pray to you. Psalm 123:1

Story to Share

Jesus and his disciples were walking in Jerusalem when they saw a blind man. Men who were blind couldn't work, so they sat by the road to beg for money.

"Jesus," asked one of his disciples, "whose fault is it that this man is blind?"

"I'd like to know, too," said another disciple. "Was it his sins or the sins of his parents that caused this man to lose his sight?"

Jesus shook his head, "Neither, my friends. This man is blind for a reason. But it has nothing to do with sin. It is so God can be praised."

Jesus spat on the ground in front of him. Mixing his spit with the dusty dirt, Jesus made a mud mixture. He bent down and picked up the cool mud in his hands. Then Jesus put the mud over the man's eyes.

"Go," he told the blind man. "Wash your eyes in the Siloam pool."

The blind man obeyed Jesus. Eagerly he washed his eyes, wondering what this meant. When the mud was gone, he brushed as much water from his eyes as he could. "I can see," he said, "I can see. Once I was blind and couldn't see, but now I can see."

The blind man thanked Jesus for giving him the joy of sight. He never wanted to use his eyes to see things that were wrong. He wanted to see Jesus and the other miracles he did. He wanted to watch Jesus as he taught the crowds. His eyes belonged to Jesus!

—*based on John 9:1–12*

Discussion Questions

1. Does Jesus love us even if we are blind or we can't hear or walk?
2. When Jesus helps us, what should we do?

Blinded Eyes Healed

Materials: • copies of this page, one for each child • scissors • glue • crayons

Preparation: Cut out pictures of blind man and sets of eyes.

Directions: Children glue the eyes to the blind man and color the picture.

What to Say: Jesus told the blind man, "Go wash your eyes in the Siloam pool." What do you think would have happened if the blind man had not obeyed? I'm sure he was glad he obeyed God! What do you think he said to his families and friends about what Jesus did for him?

Thank You, God

I look up and pray to you. Psalm 123:1

Materials: • copies of this page, one for each child • scissors • silk flowers • yarn
• green crayons • construction paper • glue • hole punch

Preparation: Cut out the flower rectangles. Remove silk flowers from stems. Cut yarn into approximately 15-inch lengths.

Directions: 1. Children color the stems and leaves. 2. Children glue the flower rectangles onto sheets of construction paper. 3. Children glue silk flowers on their papers. 4. Punch two holes at the top of each paper and tie a length of yarn to it to make a hanger.

What to Say: Think of all the beautiful things you've seen. Let's give thanks to God: **Thank you, God** (Point up with both index fingers.)**, that I can see.** (Point to eyes.) **The beautiful world** (Point out and around.) **you** (Point up.) **made for me.** (Point to self.)

Beautiful Sights!

I look up and pray to you. Psalm 123:1

Materials: • copies of this page, one for each child • small wiggle eyes, 10 for each child • glue • crayons
What to Say: Look at the beautiful flowers! If you look closely, you can see five animals looking at you.
Directions: 1. Children color the page. 2. Children glue the wiggle eyes to the animals.

Memory Verse

Pray to your Father. Matthew 6:6

Story to Share

Jesus sat on a hillside so all the people could see him. Many people came to listen to Jesus. Jesus taught people all around him. He told them about Heaven. He taught people how to be children of God. He even taught people how to pray.

Jesus said, "Don't be like some people, who pray loudly so that others will see them praying to God. Pray only to God the Father. Go to a quiet place so that you can talk to God. Don't just talk on and on and on. Remember, God knows what you need before you even ask him."

Jesus then said a prayer to show the people how to pray.

This is how you pray: Our Father in Heaven, great is your name. Please give me what I need today. Forgive me for the wrong things I have done. Help me forgive people who do wrong things to me. Help me not to do wrong things.

Then Jesus told the people we should forgive others, because God forgives us. That is how Jesus wants us to pray.

—based on Matthew 6:5–13

Discussion Questions

1. Who taught the people how to pray?
2. Whom should we pray to?
3. What does God know even before we ask him?

Hinged Picture

tape here

tape here

Materials: • copies of this page and page 187, one for each child • scissors • crayons • transparent tape

Preparation: Cut out the two strips from this page.

Directions: 1. Children color the strips you prepared and the picture from page 187. 2. Children lay the two strips on top of the full picture. Tape on either side so that the half-sections open to reveal the one underneath.

What to Say: Retell the story. Begin with showing the main scene where Jesus is teaching by folding the two flaps to the back. As you tell about the two men praying in different ways, fold the smaller flaps to the front so that they show.

Suggested Usage: Play a game in which the children copy what you do. Pray in different ways, such as sitting, standing, holding hands with others, etc. Say, **Jesus taught the people how to pray.**

Climb the Mountain

Our Father in Heaven, holy is your name. May your kingdom come and your will be done on Earth the way it is in Heaven. Give us bread to eat today. Forgive us the wrong things we do, as we forgive others who do wrong to us. Help us not to be tempted to do wrong, and save us from all bad things.

—based on Matthew 6:9–13

Materials: • copies of this page, one for each child • crayons

Directions: 1. Children draw a line through the maze to help the people reach Jesus. 2. Children color their pictures.

What to Say: **The people are climbing on the mountain to listen to Jesus. Help the people find Jesus on the mountain.** Read the Lord's Prayer aloud. **This is the prayer Jesus taught the people to say.**

188   © 2016 Rose Publishing, LLC. Permission to photocopy granted to original purchaser only. *Top 50 Instant Bible Lessons® for Preschool*

Bedtime Door Hanger

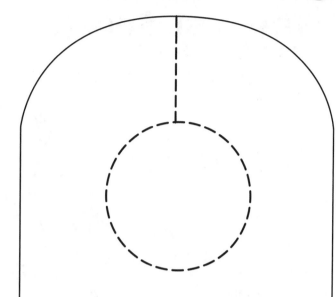

As I go to bed
each night, I will
pray to God.

Pray to your Father.
Matthew 6:6

Materials: • copies of this page, one for each child • glue • crayons
Preparation: Cut out a door hanger and a boy or girl for each child.
Directions: 1. Children color the door hanger and a boy or girl. 2. Children glue the colored child to the door hanger.
What to Say: Encourage children to hang door hangers on their bedroom door. **The children are praying before they go to sleep. God likes for us to talk to him.**

Chapter 38
The Lost Sheep

Memory Verse

Be joyful with me. I have found my lost sheep. Luke 15:6

Story to Share

Did you ever lose something that you really loved? Did it make you sad? What did you do? Of course! You looked and looked until you found it.

Jesus told a story about how much God loves and takes care of each one of us.

Pretend that you have a hundred sheep, but one day when you count your sheep, you find that one is lost. You look and look until you find that sheep. You search everywhere.

When you find your lost sheep, you would be very happy. You would say to everyone, "Come and have a party with me. I am happy that I have found my lost sheep." People that love God and are part of his family are like the sheep he had close by. The lost sheep is anyone who does not know God. Jesus will not stop helping the lost sheep find him.

God feels this way about each person. He loves everyone so much and wants to take care of them. When a person comes to know God, all of Heaven rejoices and is happy.

God wants us to be part of his family. He wants to be our Heavenly Father.

—*based on Luke 15:3–7*

Discussion Questions

1. Who told a story about a lost sheep?

2. How does God feel when one of his lost sheep is found?

Hand Puppets

Materials: • copies of this page, one for each child • transparent tape

Directions: 1. Cut out the two puppet sections. 2. Fold each section in half and tape it together.
3. Slip the Jesus puppet over your hand to tell the entire story. Slip the sheep puppet onto your other hand to tell about the lost sheep.

Bonus Idea: Make binoculars to help look for the lost sheep. Tape two bathroom tissue tubes together and cover them with construction paper. Let the children add stickers. Place pictures of sheep around the room and children use their binoculars to find them.

Lost Sheep Stand-Up

Be joyful with me. I have found my lost sheep. Luke 15:6

finished craft

Preparation: Cut on the solid lines around Jesus, keeping the dashed line intact.
Directions: 1. Children color pictures. 2. Children fold back their pictures so they will stand on their own.

Tracing Maze

Stuffed Bag Sheep

finished craft

Materials: • copies of this page, one for each child • white paper lunch bags • glue • stapler • cotton balls • old newspapers

Preparation: Cut out a sheep face a tail for each child.

Directions: 1. Children glue the sheep's face to the closed end of the bag. 2. Children wad newspaper pages and stuff them inside the bag. 3. Staple the bag closed and glue the tail at the stapled end. 4. Children glue a few cotton balls to the outside of the bag.

Chapter 39
Jesus Loves the Children

Memory Verse

I have loved you. John 15:9

Story to Share

Jesus was very different from the other religious leaders, who cared more about how they looked and acted than about the love in their hearts. Those who heard Jesus preach and watched him work miracles loved him immediately. Even when he spoke about something that was difficult for the people to hear, Jesus' eyes were filled with love.

People knew that Jesus thought children were important, too. So some parents decided to take their children to Jesus and ask him to pray for them. But when the disciples saw all the women with their small children, the disciples waved them away.

"Jesus is busy," one of them said. "Don't waste his time."

Jesus heard the disciple. In anger, he said, "Don't ever send children away from me."

Then Jesus motioned for the children to come nearer.

"See these children?" Jesus asked. "The kingdom of Heaven belongs to those who are as willing to believe as these boys and girls do. They are humble, and you will need their kind of humility to enter Heaven."

Then Jesus stretched out his arms and hugged the children to him. He laughed when he heard a tiny girl say, "Hug me, Jesus, hug me."

Jesus hugged them all. He whispered, "I love you" in their ears, and he tickled them until they giggled.

The parents smiled. They knew this was one day the boys and girls would never forget. They would always feel Jesus' arms of love around them.

—*based on Mark 10:13–16*

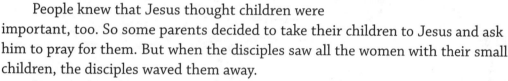

Discussion Questions

1. **Why did Jesus want to hug the children?**
2. **How does Jesus show his love for us?** (By giving us family to care for us, by giving us friends and teachers, by giving us his Word to show us the best way to live, etc.)

He Loves Me

To the tune of "Mary Had a Little Lamb."

Jesus loves me. Yes, he does!
Yes, he does. Yes, he does.
Jesus loves me. Yes, he does!
He gave me a smile.
Jesus loves you. Yes, he does!
Yes, he does. Yes, he does.
Jesus loves you. Yes, he does!
He'll give you a smile.

- -

Materials: • copies of this page, one for each child   • craft sticks   • glue   • curling ribbon
Preparation: Cut out daisies. Cut curling ribbon into lengths about 12 inches long, three for each child. Curl the ends.
Directions: 1. Children glue two daisies back to back on a craft stick. 2. Give each child three curled ribbon pieces to tie around the
top of the craft stick. 3. Sing the song to the tune of "Mary Had a Little Lamb." Children wave their daisy sticks while they sing.
What to Say: "He loves me, he loves me not" is a game that people play by pulling petals from daises. But when we think
of Jesus, we don't need to pull the petals from the daisies. We don't have to wonder if Jesus loves us. We know he does!

Sharing the Love of Jesus

Materials: • copies of this page, one for each child   • scissors   • markers or crayons   • paper bag   • transparent tape
Preparation: Cut out hearts.
Directions: 1. Children decorate their hearts in any way they wish. 2. Help children cut hearts in half. 3. Each child keeps half of a heart and puts the other half in bag. 4. Each child chooses a heart half from the bag, tapes the halves they have together, and then tries to find the child with the matching heart half.
What to Say: When you find the friend who has the heart to match the one you chose, give them a big hug and say, "Jesus loves you, and so do I!"

© 2016 Rose Publishing, LLC. Permission to photocopy granted to original purchaser only. *Top 50 Instant Bible Lessons® for Preschool*   197

Tell the Story

Materials: • copies of this page, one for each child, and one copy of page 199 • scissors • masking tape • crayons

Preparation: Cut out Jesus and children figures. Attach a piece of the stiff side of hook and loop tape to the back.
Make loops of masking tape, one for each child and one for Jesus figure. Place masking-tape loop on the back of Jesus figure
and post on a wall. (Optional: Place a sheet of butcher paper on the wall and place figures on the paper.)

Directions: 1. Children each color one of the children figures to represent themselves. 2. Help print the child's name on the picture.
3. Children place a loop of masking tape on the back of each figure. 4. Children place their figures on wall next to Jesus figure.

What to Say: Briefly retell the Bible story. **There was probably a boy who had (big blue eyes) like (Ethan) who came to Jesus.**
Continue with all the children.

Chapter 40
Timothy

 **Memory Verse**

Do what is right and fair. Proverbs 21:3

 Story to Share

Little Timothy was a happy child. Even though his father didn't believe in Jesus, Timothy's grandmother Lois and his mother, Eunice, were Christians. One of Timothy's favorite times of the day was when his mother would tell him stories about Jesus.

"Jesus took the five small loaves of bread and two dried fish from the little boy. This tiny lunch fed 5,000 people, Timothy," she said one day as she taught Timothy about Jesus' miracles.

Timothy must have wished he could have been there to see that miracle.

"Tell me another story, Mommy," Timothy begged.

As he heard his mother's stories of Jesus, Timothy realized he wanted to be a follower of Jesus.

"I believe you are the Son of God," Timothy prayed one day. "I want to belong to you."

Timothy began studying the Scriptures to learn everything he could about God. He became a follower of Jesus.

One day the missionary Paul came to visit. Paul was surprised to see how dedicated young Timothy was. Paul was impressed with Timothy's knowledge of the Scriptures and with his deep love for the stories of Jesus.

"Come with me, Timothy," Paul said. "I need a helper on my missionary journeys."

Traveling with Paul taught Timothy even more about the God he loved. Soon Paul appointed Timothy as teacher of the church at Ephesus.

One day Paul wrote Timothy a letter.

"Dear Timothy," the letter began, "don't forget the teaching and stories your mother and grandmother taught you. Be fair. Don't show favor."

Paul was Timothy's hero. Timothy knew that Paul taught only the truth. Timothy asked God to help him to be fair and to follow all of Paul's instructions to do only what was right and fair.

—based on Timothy 5

?? Discussion Questions

1. Who told Timothy to be fair?
2. How can you be fair with your friends?

Cleaning Up

Materials: • copies of this page and page 202, one of each per child • scissors • crayons • glue

Directions: 1. Cut out cleaning tools from this page, creating a set for each child. 2. Give each child a set of cleaning tools and a copy of page 202. 3. Children color the pictures. 4. Assist the children in gluing the broom in the boy's hand and the waste can beside him; the rag in the girl's hand and the spray cleaner on the table. 5. Discuss the chores that need to be done for the room to be clean again.

What to Say: How can you be fair when you and your friend made a mess? (By helping to clean up.) **When you do your share of the work, you are fair. God likes it when we are fair to each other.**

BEE-ing Fair

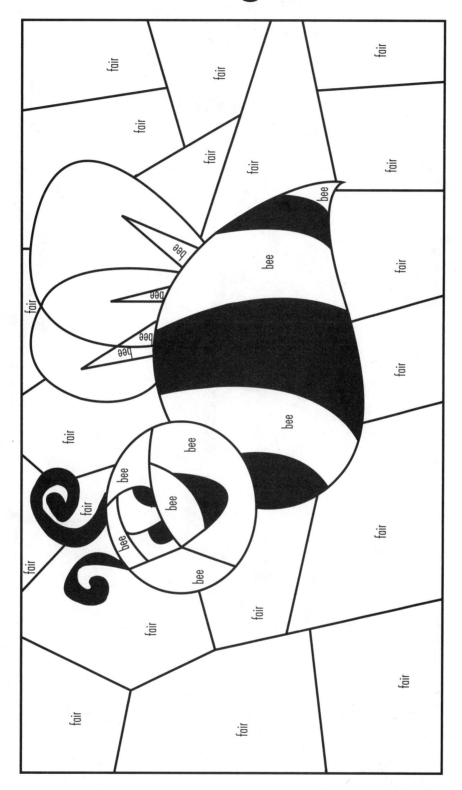

Materials: • copies of this page, one for each child • blue and yellow crayons

Directions: 1. Children color all the spaces with the word "fair" blue, and the spaces with the word "bee" yellow.

What to Say: God wants us to be fair to others. We can be fair when we take one cookie and leave another for a friend. We can be fair by taking turns to play with a toy. What are some other ways you can be fair?

Timothy's Letter

Do what is right and fair.

Proverbs 21:3

Materials: • card-stock copies of this page, one for each child • scissors • resealable plastic sandwich bags • crayons

Preparation: Cut out a puzzle for each child. Put each puzzle in a separate plastic bag.

Directions: 1. Children color their puzzles. 2. Children put together their puzzles. 3. Children place puzzles back in their bags.

What to Say: Read the verse on the puzzle. Encourage the children to repeat the verse with you as they color the puzzle and put it together. **When Timothy was a boy, God's Word was written on scrolls instead of in books like we have today. The letter Paul wrote to Timothy is in the Bible. Even though Paul wrote his letter to Timothy, God wanted it in his Word so that we can read it and learn to be fair, too.**

Memory Verse

Go. . . . Preach the good news. Mark 16:15

Story to Share

Philip was preaching in the city of Samaria. He was telling the people there about Jesus. "You can have your sins forgiven," he told them.

Many people believed what Philip told them and asked Jesus to forgive their sins. Philip was anointed by God to work many miracles. People who couldn't move were able to walk and sick people became well. The people of Samaria were very happy.

Philip enjoyed preaching to the Samaritans. It was a wonderful thing to preach and have people respond. But one day an angel appeared to Philip.

The angel said, "God wants you to leave Samaria and take the road which goes down from Jerusalem to Gaza. Take that road to the desert."

Philip didn't hesitate to obey what God said. He left right away. When he arrived at the place, Philip saw an important man from Ethiopia in a chariot. When the man came closer, Philip saw that he was reading the book from the Bible called Isaiah.

Philip ran over to the man. "Do you understand what you are reading?"

"No," answered the Ethiopian. "And I don't have anyone to tell me. Can you sit up here in my chariot and explain to me what I am reading?"

So Philip sat in the chariot and began telling the man about Jesus. "He came to earth as a baby, he was a man without sin, yet the Jews crucified him. When Jesus died on the cross, he died for your sins so that all you need to do is ask for forgiveness."

The Ethiopian man was overjoyed. "I believe," he said. "I believe that Jesus Christ is the Son of God and that he can save my sins. Thank you, Philip, for telling me the good news."

—based on Acts 8:26–39

Discussion Questions

1. What would have happened if Philip had not obeyed God?
2. Is obedience important?

Salt Painted Chariot

Go. . . . Preach
the good news.
Mark 16:15

Materials: • card-stock copies of this page, one for each child • scissors • hole punch • measuring cups • small bowls • liquid starch • water • yellow tempera paint • paintbrushes • salt • yarn **Optional:** • paint smocks

Preparation: Cut out chariots. Punch a hole in the top of chariots as indicated. Mix ¼ cup starch, ¼ cup water and two tablespoons of yellow tempera paint together. Pour the mixture into small bowls. Cut yarn into lengths approximately 6- to 8-inches long. Tie a length of yarn through the hole at the top of each chariot and tie into a loop to form a hanger.

Directions: Optional: Children put on paint smocks. 1. Children paint chariots using mixture you prepared. 2. Children sprinkle a pinch of salt over the painted chariot. 3. Set chariots aside to dry.

What to Say: Hang this in your window to remind you to tell others the good news of Jesus.

Handing Out the Good News

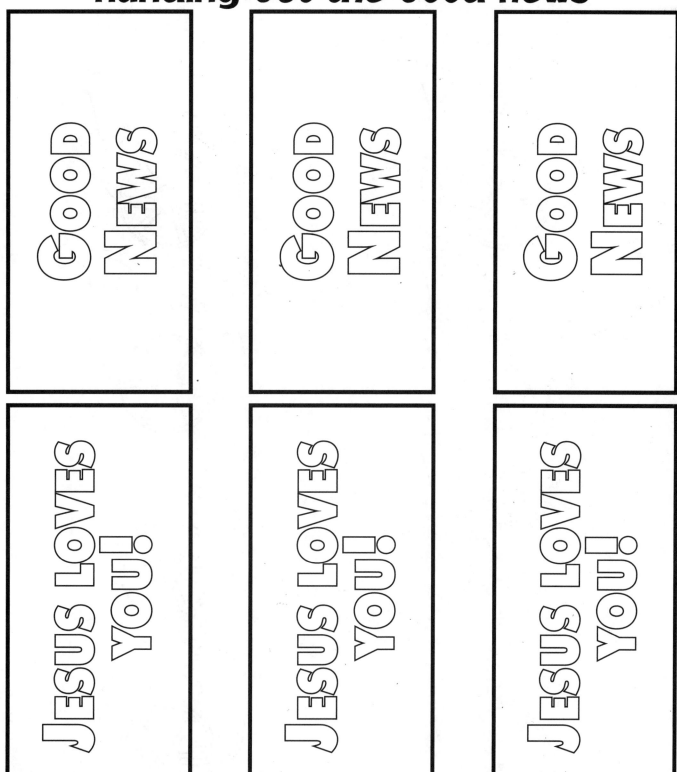

Materials: • copies of this page, one for every three children • scissors • crayons • toilet paper tubes • individually wrapped candy • tissue paper • ribbon or twist ties • crayons

Preparation: Cut out "Jesus love you!" and "Good News" tags.

Directions: 1. Each child colors a "Jesus love you!" and a "Good News" tag. 2. Children put the "Jesus loves you!" note in a toilet-paper tube along with some candy. 3. Help children wrap the tube with tissue paper and close the ends with ribbon or twist ties. 4. Children glue the "Good News" tag on the front.

What to Say: Share the good news! Give your good news gift to someone who doesn't know Jesus.

Match the Chariots

Materials: • copies of this page, one for each child • crayons

Directions: Children draw lines to connect matching chariots and color the chariots.

What to Say: We may not travel by chariot anymore, but wherever you go, you can tell people the good news about Jesus!

 Top 50 Instant Bible Lessons® for Preschool

Chariot Race

Materials: • copies of this page, one for each child • crayons • clothesline • masking tape • spring-type clothespins

Preparation: Cut out Philip figures. Stretch and secure a clothesline across the room, low enough that your preschoolers can reach it. Use masking tape to create a starting line a few feet away from the clothesline.

Directions: 1. Children color Philip. 2. Help children use clothespins to clip their Philips on the clothesline. 3. Children line up behind starting line. 4. Use stopwatch to time children as they race to clothesline, unclip their Philip, return to stand behind the starting line, hold up their Philip, and shout, "Go and preach the good news!" 5. When everyone is done, announce the time. Repeat, encouraging children to beat their previous time.

Chapter 42
The Prodigal Son

Memory Verse

Return to me. Then I will return to you. Malachi 3:7

Story to Share

A son said to his father, "Give me all my share of the family's money." He wanted to leave home and do whatever he wanted to.

So the father gave him all the money he would have gotten after the father had died. The son went far away. He lived in a way that would not please his father.

Soon, the son's money was all gone. He had nothing to eat. He had no place to live.

He went to a farmer and asked for a job feeding pigs. The son was miserable and sad. He missed his family home.

Finally, the son said, "If I go back to my father's house, at least I can ask to be a servant." The son went home. The father saw him and was filled with great joy. He ran to his son and hugged and kissed him. He threw him a big party. He forgave him.

He was just glad that he came back to him. Sometimes people don't follow God. They do things they shouldn't and look like they are running away from him.

God is happy when his children return to him. God wants to welcome us back into his family and make us his special child. All we have to do is pray and tell him we are sorry.

—*based on Luke 15:11–32*

Discussion Questions

1. When the son was hungry, what did he get a job doing? Feeding pigs.
2. How did the father feel when his son came home? He was very happy.

Forgiving Hug

God loves and forgives us just like the father forgave his lost son and gave him a hug.

Luke 15:11–32

finished craft

Materials: • copies of this page, one for each child • construction paper • glue

Preparation: Cut out face/text box images. Cut construction paper into 3x12-inch strips, making one strip for each child.

Directions: 1. Each child traces their hands on sheets of construction paper and cuts them out. 2. Copy and cut out image with writing per child. 3. Help child glue hands and image to strip of construction paper (see sketch of finished craft).

What to Say: In our story, the father gave his lost son a big hug and forgave him. God wants to forgive us when we do wrong things, too. When you do something wrong, ask God to forgive you and know that he is giving you a big hug.

Tri-Fold Pictures

Return to me. Then I will return to you. Malachi 3:7

Materials: • copies of this page, one for each child • crayons • transparent tape

Directions: 1. Each child colors the picture. 2. Help the children fold the page on the two lines that divide the scenes. 3. Tape the seams together to form a tri-fold picture. 4. Children turn the tri-fold picture to the three different scenes while you retell the story.

Go and Return Maze

There are two puzzles on this page. First help the boy go away from home. Follow the money to the farm where the pigs are. Next, follow the hearts to help the boy find his way home.

Materials: • copies of this page, one for each child • crayons

Directions: Children color pages and follow directions to draw lines along both paths.

What to Say: God loves us and wants us to be his children. Sometimes we wander away from God by sinning and doing things that do not please God. But, God is always ready to welcome us back into his arms.

A Boy Comes Home

Return to me, and I will return to you.
Malachi 3:7

finished craft

Materials: • copies of this page, one for each child • scissors • yarn • transparent tape • toilet-paper tube, one for each child • crayons

Preparation: Cut the folding "boy" picture strip and verse box from the page for each child. Cut yarn into approximately 20-inch lengths.

Directions: 1. Children color the "boy" picture strip. 2. Children fold the boy picture strip in half, sandwiching a length of yarn in the middle. 3. Tape closed the open edges opposite the fold. The yarn should move freely. 4. Children tape the verse box onto a toilet-paper tube. 5. Children thread the yarn through the tube. Help children tie the yarn ends together. 6. Demonstrate how to pull on the yarn to make the boy disappear into the tube, and then appear again.

What to Say: In our Bible story, a boy went away from home, but then he came back. When he came back, his father was happy to see him. The father gave his son a big hug! God loves us just like that father loved his son.

Memory Verse

Anyone who gives a lot will succeed. Proverbs 11:25

Story to Share

When Jesus was in Jerusalem, he loved to spend time at the temple. One day while Jesus was there he saw many people coming to the temple, bringing their offerings with them. The temple offering box hung on the wall. The top of the box was hinged and could be opened when someone wanted to give an offering.

As Jesus watched, he saw many wealthy men empty full money bags into the box. Many of the wealthy men wanted others to notice how much they were giving to God. They would wait until someone was nearby, then they would empty their bags with a flourish, making sure the coins clanged together to draw even more attention to their gifts.

Then Jesus saw a woman walking toward the box. She was a lonely widow woman who missed her husband. In Bible days, widows had very little money to buy food and clothes. Jesus saw that she carried a bit of cloth in her hands. When the woman reached the offering box, she opened the cloth she was holding. There were two small copper coins in the cloth. She placed them in the box, barely lifting her head to look around. She knew it was a small offering, but it was all she had.

Jesus' eyes were full of tears as he looked at his disciples.

"This woman's offering amounts to more than all of the offerings received today," he said.

The disciples didn't understand what Jesus meant. They had seen the two small coins, too. And they had seen the many gold coins put in by wealthy men.

"The wealthy men gave only a small portion of what they have," said Jesus. "They won't even miss the amount they gave. This woman gave God everything she had."

—based on Luke 21:1–4

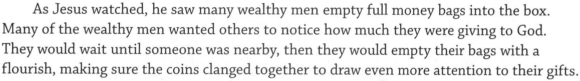

Discussion Questions

1. Do we need to give to God even if we don't have much to give?
2. What can you give to God?

Penny Poem and Verse Review

There was a little woman,
With a coin tight in her hand.
She gave it all to Jesus,
It was the best offering in the land.

Anyone who gives a lot will succeed.
Proverbs 11:25

¢

Materials: • copies of this page, one for each child • crayons • scissors • offering basket
Directions: Children color and cut out their penny pictures.
What to Say: Say the verse and choose a child to put their penny in the basket, calling the child by name. **Even when we don't have to have a lot of money to give to Jesus, he can see our generous hearts.**

Two Penny Coloring Picture

Jumpin' Pennies

¢

Materials: • 8 brown colored copies of this page • clear Con-Tact paper • scissors

Directions: 1. Write each word from the memory verse on a separate penny and the scripture reference on the eighth penny. 2. Cover the pennies with clear Con-Tact paper and cut them out. 3. Lay the pennies on the floor, approximately 2 feet (jumping distance) apart. 4. Children take turns jumping from penny to penny as you say the words to the verse.

Suggested Usage: Use this activity when you have a few extra minutes of class time. Not only will it help to get rid of some wiggles, it will reinforce the verse in their minds.

Penny Puzzle Pass

Materials: • copies of this page, one for each child • scissors • resealable plastic sandwich bags • crayons • large paper bag

Preparation: Cut out puzzle pieces. Place the pieces from each puzzle in a separate plastic bag.

Directions: 1. Children color their puzzle pieces. As children work, circulate and print each child's name on the back of their puzzle pieces. 2. When finished, children place all their pieces in a large paper bag. 3. Children sit in a circle and pass the bag around. When the bag comes to them, children take one puzzle piece out of it. 4. If a child draws a piece they already have, they should return the piece to the bag and choose another. 5. Give each child an envelope to take their new puzzle pieces home.

Chapter 44

Samaritan Woman at the Well

Memory Verse

A friend loves at all times. Proverbs 17:17

Story to Share

Jesus was taking a trip. He was going from Samaria to Judea. Jesus' disciples were with him. "I'm getting hungry," one of them said.

"Let's rest here," said Jesus, pointing to a well. "We can get some food and drink."

Jesus' disciples went into the town to get some food. Jesus sat down on the edge of the well to rest and wait. A Samaritan woman came to the well to get some water.

"Hi!" said Jesus. "I'm thirsty. Could you give me a drink of water?"

The woman was surprised that Jesus talked to her. "Why are you talking to me? You are a Jew and Jews don't talk to Samaritans." She had never met him before but he knew many things about her life. She was amazed.

Jesus knew everyone was important to God, no matter who they were, what they looked like or what they owned. Not only did he drink the water she gave to him, Jesus also told her how to be saved.

This woman was so excited she hurried to town. "Come and see!" she said. "Jesus is here."

Because Jesus was friendly to one woman, many others came and learned how to be saved. Jesus knows all about your life too. You are important to him. He wants you to be in his family.

—based on John 4:1–39

Discussion Questions

1. Do you like it when others are friendly to you?

2. When can you be friendly to others?

Hello at the Well

Materials: • copies of this page and page 222, one of each for each child • scissors • glue • paper fasteners • crayons

Preparation: Cut out the pieces for each child.

Directions: 1. Children color the pieces. 2. Children glue Jesus to the well so that it looks like he is sitting on the well. 3. Help children push brads through the arms and Jesus' body as indicated.

What to Say: Look, you can see how friendly Jesus is by waving his arm. Can you wave your arm and let someone know you are friendly? Do you think Jesus was friendly to everyone or only a few people? Jesus didn't choose to be friends with only the people who had lots of money, or those who were beautiful. He was friendly to everyone. Jesus wans us to be friendly to everyone, too!

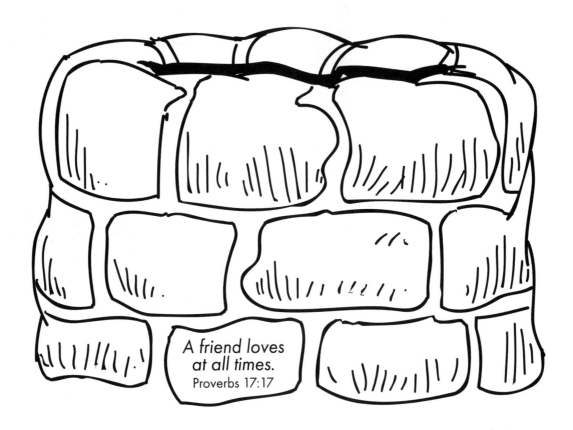

A friend loves
at all times.
Proverbs 17:17

Friendly Children

A friend loves at all times.
Proverbs 17:17

- -

Materials: • card-stock copies of this page, one for each child • scissors • resealable plastic sandwich bags • crayons
Preparation: Cut out a puzzle for each child.
Directions: 1. Children color puzzles, using as many different colors as possible. 2. Help children as needed as they cut puzzle pieces out and the reassemble the puzzles as time allows. 3. Children place their puzzle pieces in a plastic bag to take home.
What to Say: Who do you think is friendly? Are only children from the United States friendly? What about Russian children? Latin-American children? God will help all his children to be friendly.

Jesus at the Well

Materials: • card-stock copies of this page, one for each child and one extra • scissors • resealable plastic sandwich bags
• crayons • glue • craft sticks

Preparation: Cut out the story pictures. Place each set of pictures in a separate plastic bag. Follow directions below to make a set of picture sticks.

Directions: Children color the pictures and then glue each one to a craft stick.

What to Say: Retell the Bible story, holding up the appropriate picture stick at each part of the story. Lead children to hold up their picture sticks with you.

Memory Verse

Let the peace that Christ gives rule in your hearts. Colossians 3:15

Story to Share

Everyone wanted to see Jesus. Word had spread that Jesus was coming through Jericho. Excitement filled the air as men and women tried to push through the crowd so they could be sure to see Jesus.

One little, short man named Zacchaeus tried to push his way through the crowd. I'll never be able to see over everyone, he thought to himself. "If only I were taller," he said out loud as people deliberately blocked his way. But it wasn't only his size that kept people from letting him through. Nobody liked Zacchaeus.

Zacchaeus was a tax collector. He was very rich because he collected money for the Romans. Then Zacchaeus would make the taxpayers pay extra to him. Zacchaeus was growing rich because he was cheating others.

Zacchaeus was frustrated when everywhere he turned seemed blocked so he decided to see Jesus another way. He climbed up in one of the big sycamore trees that were planted along the road to provide shade for tired travelers. "Now I can see," he said. Sure enough, there was Jesus walking down the dusty road. Closer and closer Jesus walked. He looks so kind, Zacchaeus thought. I wonder if he would love a sinner like me?

Just then Jesus stopped under the tree where Zacchaeus was sitting. Zacchaeus was so surprised he nearly fell out of the tree! "Zacchaeus," said Jesus in a soft, kind voice. "Come down out of the tree. I want to go to your house."

Jesus wasn't at his house very long until Zacchaeus knew that Jesus loved him. He was so happy he said, "Jesus, take my heart. I want to belong to you. I will not only give back the money I have taken from people, but I will give them back four times the amount."

Jesus was happy too. "Today a man has been saved!" he said.

—*based on Luke 19:1–10*

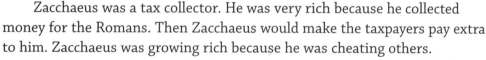

Discussion Questions

1. How did Jesus know that Zacchaeus was in the tree?
2. Did Zacchaeus's size matter to Jesus? Why?

Memory Verse Review

Materials: • one copy of this page • scissors • crayons • markers

Preparation: Cut out and color the cards.

Directions: 1. Divide the class into four groups. Give each group a card. 2. Say, **These cards will help us say the memory verse. The first group has lettuce to help us remember "let." The second group has Jesus, which helps us remember "Christ." The third group has a ruler to help us remember "rule." The fourth group has the hearts. What will that help us remember?** 3. Have each group stand and say their word, filling in with "the peace of" and "in your." 4. Form new groups and redistribute the cards. Repeat as time and interest allow.

In My Heart

finished craft

Materials: • copies of this page, two for each child • scissors • hole punch • yarn • transparent tape

Preparation: Cut out hearts and Jesus picture. Punch out holes as indicated on each heart. Cut a length of yarn approximately 12-inches long for each child. Wrap one end of each yarn length with tape. Placing two hearts back-to-back, thread the unwrapped end of a length of yarn through the top left hole and tie a knot. Continue tying pairs of hearts until you have one pair for each child.

Directions: 1. Give each child a pair of hearts and a Jesus picture. 2. Demonstrate how to sew around the edges of the heart. 3. When each child has finished sewing around the edges, help tie a knot at the end. 4. Give each child a Jesus picture to put in the heart.

What to Say: When you are tempted to disobey your parents, break something, or say something mean, take the head of Jesus out of your heart and remember: "Let the peace of Christ rule in your heart" (Colossians 3:15).

Giving Hearts

To the tune of "The Ants Go Marching."

The children go marching one by one. Hurrah! Hurrah!
The children go marching one by one. Hurrah! Hurrah!
The children go marching one by one
Giving their hearts to God's only Son.
And they all go marching down
To the ground
To get out of the rain.
Boom! Boom! Boom!

My heart belongs to Jesus.

_____

- -

Materials: • copies of this page, one for each child • scissors • crayons • paper doilies • glue • index cards
Preparation: Cut out hearts.
Directions: 1. Help children print their name on the blank line on the heart. 2. Children glue the heart to the paper doily.
What to Say: This heart says, "My heart belongs to Jesus." When we love someone, we say we give our hearts to them. Saying our hearts belong to Jesus, it is a way to say that we love Jesus. Make a large circle with the children. Sing the song above to the tune of "The Ants Go Marching." On the appropriate line, children lay their hearts in the middle of the circle.

Hang On Tight

Hang on tight, we're climbing the tree.
Up, up, up, it's Jesus we'll see.
Hang on tight, we're up so high,
We can almost touch the sky.

Hang on tight; Jesus is here!
He says, "Come, and have no fear."
Hang on tight, we're moving fast.
Down, down, down, on the ground at last.

Materials: • copies of this page, one for each child • crayons
Directions: Children color the picture as you read the poem.
What to Say: Lead children to do with the following motions with you as you read the poem again. Start the poem with your hands on the floor. Then keep stretching and climbing as you say the first stanza until you "almost touch the sky." On the second stanza, move back down slowly until your hands are back on the floor.

Chapter 46
Jesus Is Baptized

 Memory Verse

How beautiful are the feet of those who bring good news! Romans 10:15

Story to Share

"I have something to tell you," said John the Baptist as he wandered from place to place. John the Baptist was Jesus' cousin. God had given John a very important message to tell to the people.

As the crowds sat on the river bank listening to him preach, John said, "What I have to tell you is that you need to get ready. Get ready for the one who is coming soon. Turn from your sin. The Kingdom of Heaven will soon be here."

John's words were different from what the people had heard before. Everything about John was different. He wore clothes that were roughly woven from camel's hair and held together with a leather belt. He ate dried grasshoppers dipped in wild honey he found in the trees. Many thought he was strange, but many believed and turned from their wickedness.

"Repent, repent from your sins," John preached. And as people repented, John baptized them in the Jordan River.

"I'm baptizing you with water," said John, "but this King who comes after me is so good and pure, I am not even worthy to unfasten his sandals."

One day while John was baptizing those who had listened to his words and repented, John looked up to see Jesus waiting to be baptized. This was the one he had been preaching about. This was the King he had said was coming.

"I can't baptize you, Jesus," said John. "You are too pure and good."

"No," said Jesus. "My Father, God, wants us all to be baptized to show that we believe in him."

John obeyed Jesus and baptized him in the Jordan River. When he did, the sky opened and the Holy Spirit, taking on the form of a dove, appeared and the voice of God could be heard. "This is my Son and I love him," said God. "He pleases me."

John continued telling others the good news of Jesus.

—based on Matthew 3:1–17

?? Discussion Questions

1. Does everyone want to hear about Jesus?
2. Who first told you about Jesus? Make sure you say thank you to them.

Beautiful Feet

_____

will tell
the good
news of
Jesus

Materials: • butcher paper • paint of different colors • paper towels
Directions: 1. Cut the butcher paper into 1x1-foot pieces. 2. Paint the bottom of each foot on the child and put the imprint on the page. 3. Write the child's name and then the words, "will tell the good news of Jesus."
What to Say: God wants us to go and tell people about Jesus. We can use our feet to go and tell people about Jesus.
Alternate Idea: Instead of using paint, copy the sample above for children to color and print their names on.

John's Clothes

Materials: • card-stock copies of this page, one for each child plus one extra • scissors • instant coffee granules
• 9x13-inch pan • glue • shallow bowls • paint brushes • transparent tape

Preparation: Cut out John and clothes, one set per child and one extra for you to use in demonstrating the craft. Pour the coffee in the pan.
Pour glue into bowls.

Directions: 1. Children brush glue on John's coat. 2. Demonstrate how to lay the coat in the coffee, glue side down, then shake off excess
coffee. 3. Demonstrate how to place the coat on John figure and fold the tabs back. 4. Place tape to secure the coat to each John figure.

What to Say: What you wear isn't important to Jesus. John wore a coat of camel's hair. But he pleased Jesus by
telling others about him. Jesus will be pleased with you if you use your feet to go tell your friends about him.

Kind Feet

Materials: • copies of this page, one for each child • crayons

Directions: Children color the pictures of those with kind feet and cross out those with unkind feet.

What to Say: Can you think of a time that you used your feet to be kind? Draw a picture of it in the last box.

Shoe Match

Chapter 47

Jesus Enters Jerusalem

Memory Verse

Hosanna! . . . Blessed is the king! John 12:13

Story to Share

There were many people in Jerusalem. They had come to the Passover feast. This is when all the Jewish people came together to celebrate special things God had done for them.

Jesus knew it was time to go to Jerusalem. When he was close to the town, he asked his disciples to go get a donkey that would be waiting for them and bring it back.

When the people heard that Jesus was coming to Jerusalem, they were very excited. They had heard all the amazing things Jesus had done. Some believed he was God's Son, some believed he was a great teacher.

A big crowd laid their coats on the ground in front of where Jesus would walk on the donkey. Others cut branches from the trees and spread them on the road. They held palm branches to wave. Many people lined up along the streets to see Jesus.

Soon, Jesus rode into the city on the donkey. The people shouted, "Hosanna! Blessed is the king!" They praised Jesus and waved the palm branches. Then they shouted some more, "Hosanna! Blessed is the king!"

It meant that they were excited and joyful that he was there. They believed Jesus would save them from all the bad leaders that made their life hard. Jesus was there to help them be close to God.

—*based on John 12:12–15*

Discussion Questions

1. What did people wave when Jesus came into town?
2. What did the people shout?
3. Who is the king?
4. What was Jesus riding on?

Praising Jesus

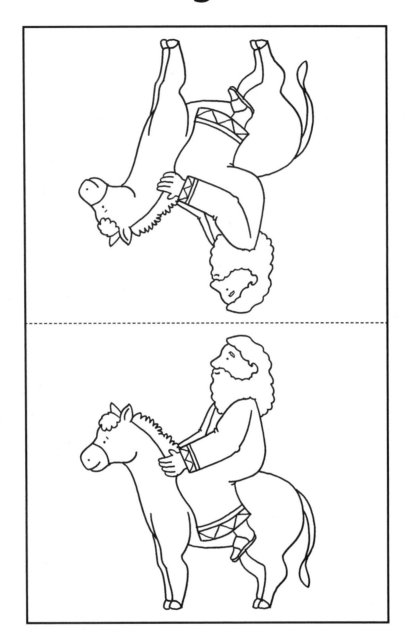

Materials: • copies of this page, one for each child plus one extra • scissors • crayons

Preparation: Cut out folding pictures of Jesus and palm leaves. Follow directions below to prepare a set of pictures to use as an example.

Directions: 1. Children color folding pictures of Jesus and two palm leaves. 2. Children fold the picture in half at the dashed lines to make a Jesus stand-up.

What to Say: Retell the Bible story, moving the Jesus stand-up along a table. Ask children to place their palm leaves on the table for Jesus to "ride" on. Retell story again as children reenact the story with you.

Another Idea: Attach a length of crepe paper to the front of each Jesus stand-up. Children pull their Jesus stand-ups around the room. **Jesus came to Jerusalem riding on a donkey. The people praised him.**

Hosanna! . . . Blessed is the king! John 12:13

Spinning Praiser

Hosanna! . . . Blessed is the king!

John 12:13

Materials: • copies of this page, one for each child • scissors • crayons • paper-towel tubes • green paper • transparent tape

Preparation: Cut out the verse strips. For each child, cut four strips approximately 1x11-inches long from green paper for each child.

Directions: 1. Children use crayons to decorate verse strips and paper-towel tubes. 2. Children tape each strip of green paper to the top edge of the tube. Bend each strip back a little, so they point outward. 3. Children tape the verse strip around the tube, about halfway up. 4. Demonstrate how to roll the tube between hands to make it spin.

What to Say: See how the praiser spins? We can use our spinning praisers to praise Jesus.

Praise Puzzle

Hosanna! . . . Blessed is the king! John 12:13

Materials: • copies of this page, one for each child   • crayons   • resealable plastic sandwich bags   • clear Con-Tact paper

Directions: 1. As the children color the picture, read the verse to them. 2. Cover the puzzles with clear Con-Tact paper and cut them apart at the dashed lines. 3. Help the children reassemble their puzzles. 4. Give each child plastic bag to carry home the puzzle.

Chapter 48
Jesus Is Crucified

Memory Verse

He forgave us all our sins. Colossians 2:13

Story to Share

When people sinned, God was sad. He knew the only way their sins could be forgiven was for a sinless man to die in place of them. That's why God sent his Son, Jesus, to earth as a tiny baby. He knew Jesus would grow up and be the sinless man who could die for the sins of all people.

Jesus did many wonderful miracles while he was on earth. He taught about his Father, God. He preached love, forgiveness, and joy. He loved everyone, not just the wealthy or beautiful, but also the poor, the disfigured, and even those who hated him.

One day those men who hated Jesus nailed him to a cross. They beat Jesus, spat in his face, put thorns on his head like a crown and then put nails through his hands and feet. How Jesus suffered! But the words he spoke remind us how sinless he was.

"Father, forgive them," Jesus prayed as he hung on the cross.

When Jesus died, they put him in a tomb. His mother, Mary, was sad. His disciples were sad. Those who loved him and believed he was the Son of God were sad. But they didn't know the secret.

Three days later, Jesus rose from the dead. Soldiers had sealed the stone on the tomb so nobody could steal his body—but that didn't keep him inside. Jesus rose from the grave and is alive today!

And now, because Jesus died, we can be forgiven from our sins. Jesus wants us to believe he is the Son of God. He wants us to tell him our sins. Then Jesus is ready to forgive us. He is our Savior.

—*based on Matthew 27:32—28:10*

Discussion Questions

1. **What did the men do to Jesus that caused him to ask God to forgive the men?** (Beat him, spit on him, crucified him, etc.)
2. **What will Jesus forgive you for?** (Disobeying, selfishness, unloving attitudes, etc.)

Cross Sun Catcher

Materials: • one copy of this page • cardboard • scissors • ribbon • clear Con-Tact paper
• colored paper • heart punch • glitter • permanent marker

Preparation: Cut out and trace the cross to cardboard for a pattern. Cut out cross pattern. Cut ribbon into lengths 6- to 8-inches long.

Directions: 1. Children punch hearts from different colors of paper. 2. Give each child two 4x8-inch pieces of clear Con-Tact paper. 3. Peel the paper from one side of each child's Con-Tact paper and place it on the table, sticky side up. 4. Children press the colored hearts on the sticky side of the plastic. 5. Assist the children in sprinkling glitter over the hearts. 6. Go around and peel the paper off each child's second square and press on top of the first. 7. Using a permanent marker and the cross template, trace a cross on each child's plastic and cut it out. 8. Children punch holes at the tops of their crosses. 8. Help children tie lengths of ribbon through the crosses to make loops for hanging.

What to Say: God gave his Son, Jesus, to die for our sins because he loves us. Jesus was willing to die because he loves us, too. The hearts in your cross will remind you of his love. How can you show your love for God and Jesus?

Scene in a Cup

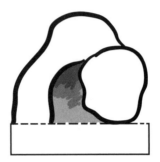

He forgave us
all our sins.
Colossians 2:13

Materials: • copies of this page, one for each child   • scissors   • crayons   • 8-ounce foam cups   • glue   • tiny silk flowers

Preparation: Cut out cross circles, tombs, and verse rectangles.

Directions: 1. Children color a cross circle, tomb, and verse rectangle. 2. Help children glue the cross circle to the inside bottom of a cup.
3. Children fold the tab on the tomb and glue it to the wall of the cup, about halfway down the cup. Make sure cross picture at bottom of cup is upright. 4. Children glue the verse rectangles on the outsides of the cups. 5. Let the children glue silk flowers inside cups, near the tombs.

What to Say: Jesus died as a sinless offering for our sins. But Jesus didn't stay dead! He arose from the grave and is living today!

I'm Forgiven Wristlet

I'm forgiven!

I'm forgiven!

I'm forgiven!

Materials: • copies of this page, one for every three children • crayons • small stickers • transparent tape

Preparation: Cut out wristlets.

Directions: 1. Children color their wristlets. 2. Children decorate their wristlets with small stickers.

3. Fit each child's wristlet to their wrist, fastening with clear tape. Cut off the excess paper.

What to Say: Our wristlets have the words "I'm forgiven!" written on them. When you wear your wristlet, you can remember that Jesus forgives our sins when we ask him. It will also remind you that Jesus wants us to forgive others.

Sort and Learn

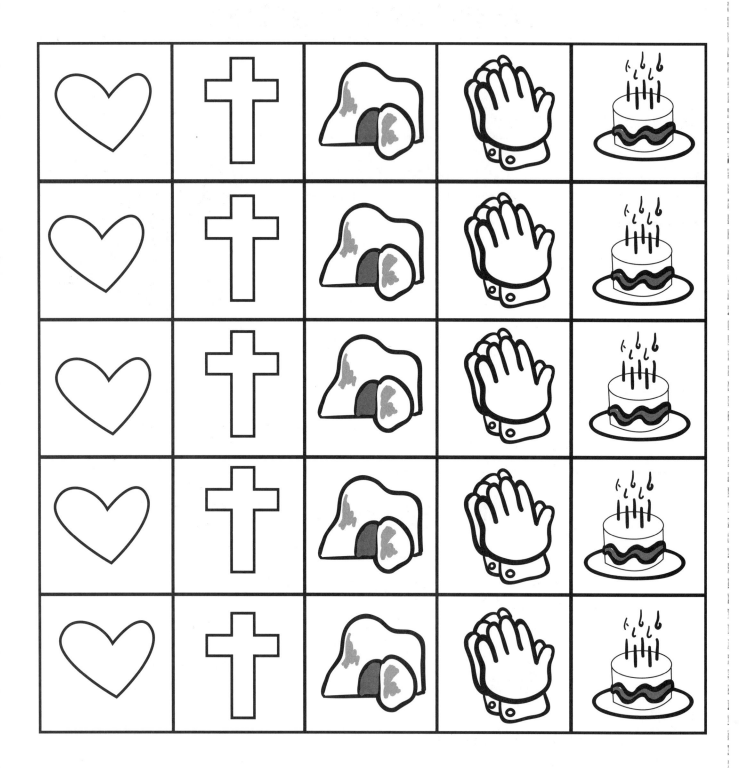

Materials: • copies of this page, one for every five children • crayons • scissors
Directions: 1. Children color the pictures. 2. As needed, help children cut the squares apart.
What to Say: Let's find all of our cut-out hearts and place them in a pile. God sent his Son, Jesus, to Earth because he loves us. Let's find our crosses. Jesus died on the cross so our sins could be forgiven. Let's find our tombs. Jesus arose from the dead. He's alive! Let's find our praying hands. We can ask Jesus to forgive our sins. Let's find our party cakes. We can celebrate Jesus' forgiveness.

Chapter 49
Jesus' Resurrection

 Memory Verse

You are the light of the world. Matthew 5:14

 Story to Share

The people who loved Jesus were sad. They had watched as Jesus' body was put in a tomb. Afterward, Jesus' friends went home to cry.

Three days later on Sunday morning, Mary Magdalene and some other women walked to the tomb where Jesus was buried. They brought spices to put in the tomb so it would smell good.

Imagine their surprise when they found it empty! Not only did they find an empty tomb, they found an angel there to greet them.

The women stared at the shining angel.

"He is not here, he is alive!" the angel said, pointing to the grave clothes in the tomb.

"Go," the angel said. "Go and tell Jesus' disciples that he has risen."

For a moment, the women could only stare at the angel. Then they turned and began walking back toward town. Faster and faster they walked until they gathered up their skirts and ran. The expensive spices they carried fell to the ground as they ran.

Seeing Peter, the women stopped. At first he couldn't understand what they were trying to tell him. They were so excited that they spoke all at once!

"Stop, slow down," Peter said. "Just one of you speak."

Mary Magdalene clutched at his arm. "It's Jesus," she said. "He's not dead. He's not in the grave. He's alive!"

Peter stared at her. "What?" he asked in astonishment.

"It's true," Mary said with a joyful laugh. "Come and see!"

—*based on John 20:1–18*

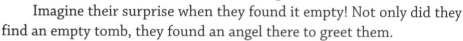 **Discussion Questions**

1. **What exciting news did Mary tell Peter about Jesus?** (Jesus is alive!)
2. **What exciting news can you tell your friends about Jesus?** (He loves them. He will forgive their sins.)

Come and See

Materials: • copy of this page and page 247, one of each • scissors • crayons • masking tape

Preparation: Use masking tape to make a long line on the floor. Make a second masking-tape line a few feet from the first, a third line a few feet from the second, and a final line a few feet from the third. You will have made three separate sections.

Directions: 1. Place the pictures and crayons on a table to be colored by kids who arrive early. 2. Before playing game, place the tomb on the floor in the first section, the angel in the second, and Mary in the third. 3. Children stand facing the first section. When you say, "Jesus died," the children jump in the section with the tomb. When you say, "He's not here," the children jump to the angel's section. When you say, "Come and see," the children jump to Mary's section. 4. For later rounds, mix up the order of the commands or vary their motion (walk on tiptoes, hop on one foot, crawl, etc.).

What to Say: We didn't live when Jesus was on Earth. We didn't get to see the angel that announced he had risen from the dead. But we can go and tell others it happened. We can invite them to come to church with us and worship.

Story Sequence Worksheet

Materials: • copies of this page, one for each child plus one extra • construction paper • scissors • stapler • masking tape • crayons • glue

Preparation: Cut construction paper into 4½x6-inch rectangles, making five rectangles for each child plus five extra. Staple five construction-paper rectangles together to make a book. Cover the staples with tape to prevent injury. Make one construction-paper book for each child. Follow the directions below to make a sample book.

Directions: 1. Children color the pictures. 2. Children cut the pictures apart and glue them in the books. 3. Children "read" their books.

What to Say: Discuss the pictures. As you retell the Bible story, ask children to point to each picture in turn. Show them your book so they can copy the numbers, and put their pages in the correct order.

Shining Your Light

Materials: • copies of this page, one for each child • crayons
Directions: 1. Children color the pictures of the children who are letting their lights shine. 2. Children draw an X on those who are not letting their lights shine.
What to Say: One at a time, discuss each picture. **Does it look like the boy [or girl] is shining for Jesus? When you are mean to others, they don't know you belong to Jesus. But when you are kind and caring, they know you are different—you want to be like Jesus!**

Chapter 50
Jesus Goes Home to Heaven

Memory Verse

[Jesus] has prepared a city. Hebrews 11:16

Story to Share

One day while Jesus was teaching his disciples, he told them about Heaven. He said, "Where my Father lives are many mansions. I am going to prepare one for you."

"But wait a minute," Thomas said to Jesus. "Are you saying we have to find our own way to Heaven?"

"No," Jesus answered. "I am the way to Heaven. If you believe I am the Son of God, then you also know my Father."

His friends didn't understand what Jesus was saying. But they did know that they believed Jesus was the Son of God.

Soon it was time for Jesus to return to his Father in Heaven. His friends watched as he went up, up, up into the sky. They stared until he disappeared behind the clouds. While the disciples were still looking up to the sky where Jesus had disappeared into the clouds, they heard a voice. Two angels were watching them.

"Don't be sad," the angels told the disciples. "Jesus is coming back one day to take you, and all those who believe he is the Son of God, to Heaven with him."

Later Jesus' friend John had a dream about Heaven. He saw thousands and thousands of angels singing praise songs to God. He saw beautiful palaces and golden streets.

The vision made John want to be with Jesus in Heaven even more. John knew that Heaven would be a perfect place with no sadness or pain. So he spent the rest of his life telling people how wonderful Heaven would be. He even wrote a book about it. That book is the last one in the Bible. It is called "Revelation."

—*based on John 14:1–14, Acts 1:1–11, Revelation*

Discussion Questions

1. **What do you think Heaven is like?** (Beautiful, shiny, angels, fun, etc.)
2. **How can you be ready for Heaven?** (Believe Jesus is God's Son and confess your sins.)

What's in Heaven?

Materials: • copies of this page, one for each child • crayons

Directions: 1. Children use their yellow crayon to color the things they will find in Heaven.

2. Children use their green crayon to color the things they will not find in Heaven.

What to Say: Why won't we find a lamp in Heaven? (Because Jesus will shine.) Discuss the other pictures. **We can look forward to living in Jesus' home forever.**

Jesus Goes Home

Materials: • copies of pages 252 and 253, one Jesus figure and one scene picture for each child
• scissors • yarn • ruler • crayons • transparent tape

Preparation: Cut out a Jesus picture for each child. Cut slits on the dashed lines on the
scene pictures. Cut yarn into 12-inch lengths, making one for each child.

Directions: 1. Children color the pictures. 2. Assist each child in taping a Jesus to a length of yarn and threading the yarn through the
slits, pulling tight. Tape the ends together. 3. Show how to pull the yarn on the back of the picture to move Jesus up in the sky.

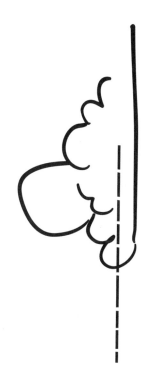

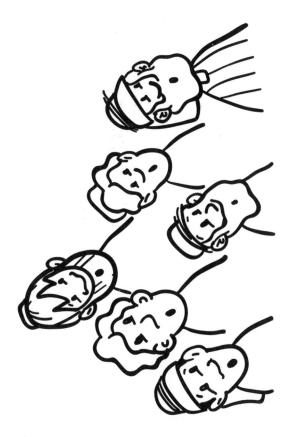

Seeing Jesus and His Home

Materials: • card-stock copies of this page, one for each child • scissors • craft foam • pipe cleaners • markers • hole punch

Preparation: Using the card stock pattern, cut foam eyeglasses for each child. Punch a hole in the top of each corner.

Directions: 1. Children decorate their glasses with markers. 2. Each child twists a pipe cleaner into each hole. Help them curve the ends like ear pieces. Go around and cut off the excess. 3. Children put on their glasses.

What to Say: Can you imagine seeing Jesus and his Home? The Bible tells us to watch for when he comes back to take us to Heaven. We can watch for Jesus by obeying his Word and keeping our hearts free from sin.

R✹SEKiDZ® RESOURCES FOR TEACHERS

Look for more great titles in our popular Top 50 Instant Bible Lessons series!
Here are some favorites:

Top 50 Instant Bible Lessons for Elementary
AGES 5–10, 252 PAGES, PAPERBACK

Enjoy having a whole year's worth of Bible lessons at your fingertips! The *Top 50 Instant Bible Lessons for Elementary* cover the top 50 Bible stories and includes BONUS lessons for Christmas and Easter. Includes reproducible hand-outs, arts and crafts templates, puzzles, games, and step-by-step instructions.

Product Code: R50003
ISBN: 978-1-62862-498-4

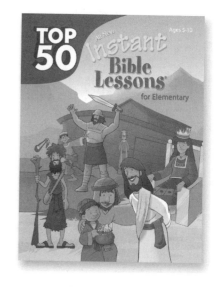

Top 50 Object Lessons: Games & Activities
AGES 5–10, 208 PAGES, PAPERBACK

The easy-to-follow, volunteer-friendly book *Top 50 Bible Object Lessons* creates opportunities for children to remember the main theme using science and everyday objects. Teach kids key Bible stories plus twenty bonus holiday and favorite game object lessons. Quick and easy-to-use for Sunday School, midweek programs, homeschool and more! Includes reproducible pages.

Product Code: R50009
ISBN: 978-1-62862-504-2

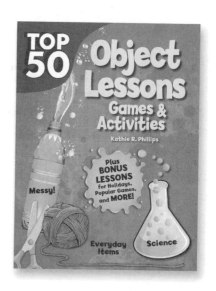

Top 50 Memory Verse Lessons: with Games & Activities
AGES 5–10, 208 PAGES, PAPERBACK

Memory verses are vital to hiding God's Word in the heart and mind of every child. *Top 50 Memory Verses with Games & Activities* makes verse memorization easy! Kids will have so much fun, they won't realize they're memorizing Scripture. The book is packed with fun, interactive, creative, and engaging ways to get children excited about Scripture.

Product Code: R50010
ISBN: 978-1-62862-505-9

To order books, contact customerservice@hendricksonrose.com. To talk live to a Customer Service Representative, call 800-358-3111, 8:30AM - 5:00PM, EST

ROSEKiDZ® RESOURCES FOR TEACHERS

Big Puzzles for Little Hands: The Bible Tells Me So
AGES 3–8, 96 PAGES, PAPERBACK

Young children are very inquisitive and love to learn new things—the most important of which are Bible truths. With *Big Puzzles for Little Hands,* you can provide that scriptural instruction using fun, age-based activities that kids love. From mazes to color-by-number to seek-and-find, these puzzles will help even the smallest children learn more about God's love and his plan for their lives. Over 80 lessons from the Old and New Testaments! Every lesson includes: Memory verse; Bible story reference; tips for teacher talk; easy instruction; reproducible pages.

Product Code: R36834
ISBN: 978-1-88535-880-6

The Super-Sized Book of Bible Puzzles
AGES 5–10, 256 PAGES, PAPERBACK

Fun Bible learning with pencils and crayons! *The Super-Sized Book of Bible Puzzles* has over 210 fun searches, mazes, pictures, and puzzles that help kids learn their favorite Bible stories from the Old and New Testaments. It is perfect for families, Sunday school teachers, home schools, and Christian school leaders. Answers included.

Product Code: R38251
ISBN: 978-1-58411-142-9

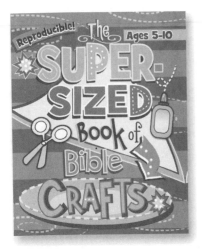

The Super-Sized Book of Bible Crafts
AGES 5–10, 256 PAGES, PAPERBACK

The Super-Sized Book of Bible Crafts is perfect for use at home, in church, or in Sunday School. Designed for children ages 5 to 10 years, this reproducible book is jam-packed with fun crafts and exciting projects that help children to better understand God's Word. Each project includes clear directions on how to build each craft using simple, everyday household items and materials. Includes a craft index by theme in the back.

Product Code: R38252
ISBN: 978-1-58411-150-4

To order books, contact customerservice@hendricksonrose.com. To talk live to a Customer Service Representative, call 800-358-3111, 8:30AM - 5:00PM, EST